Dream Flights

INTERNATIONAL

ASK ABOUT OUR PLUS CARD

https://www.dreamflightsintl.com/

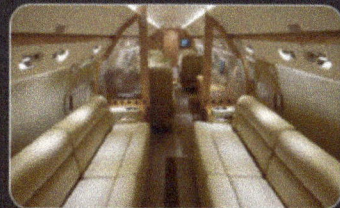

RAMCIEL MAGAZINE

CONTENTS

23 AFRICAN ROOTS

27 CONTINUING THE LEGACY

Bol Manute Bol being drafted into the NBA as I'm very far away to be able to celebrate with the family

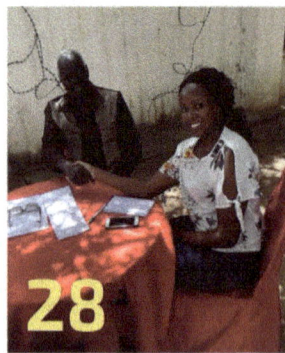

28 GEN. GEORGE KONGOR

From 1991 to 1994 he was the governor of Bahr el Ghazal, and from 1994 to 2000 he was the second Vice President of Sudan

RAMCIEL MAGAZINE

CONTENTS

RAMCIEL MAGAZINE'S SECOND EDITION EDITORIAL

Deng Mayik Atem

Dear Friends of Ramciel,

It had been quite an experience in terms of convincing people to give interviews, writing the article, and providing photos for the publishing. But with all efforts and willingness of our people, we did manage to obtain credible content for this beautiful publication, and hopefully, you won't be disappointed browsing and reading through this lecture.

This second edition hardcopy of Ramciel Magazine and the first ever to have been printed in the country will introduce Ramciel to the population of South Sudan. This new magazine has one goal, to encourage the people of South Sudan—especially those of us in the Diaspora, those of us who are living not only in the United States but throughout the world—to celebrate our nation and our culture.

ALTHOUGH OUR PEOPLE ARE FROM 64 TRIBES PLUS ARABS AND SOME WHITES, WE HAVE FAR MORE IN COMMON THAN WE HAVE SEPARATED US.

Although our people are from 64 tribes plus Arabs and some Whites, we have far more in common than we have separated us. The most important thing we have in common is a love for our homeland. Ramciel Magazine is intended to celebrate us as a people and to help us to discuss the important issues and problems that need to be addressed as South Sudan moves forward.

Two years ago, an idea was born to create a magazine for the South Sudanese diaspora, a magazine that would speak to the interests of South Sudanese people who are scattered around the globe.

Of course, we will also be happy to sign you up for a subscription to Ramciel, which means that you can look forward to the editions yet to come. For those who have businesses and would like to advertise in Ramciel Magazine, we have a variety of low-priced alternatives, which we will happily discuss with you.

This will bring your businesses to the attention not only to the members of the Diaspora but also to our readers here. At first, it was an online magazine, but from the beginning, we wanted both an electronic and a print presence. That idea has been realized; Ramciel Magazine is a reality, and that is why we are celebrating.

WE SHALL LOOK FORWARD TO RAMCIEL'S THIRD EDITION HARD COPY THAT WILL BE DUE IN -APRIL MAY 2020.

That is why we are celebrating our second edition this year, and we shall look forward to Ramciel's Third edition hard copy that will be due in -April May 2020. Of course, we will also be happy to sign you up for a subscription to Ramciel, which means that you can look forward to the editions yet to come.

For those who have businesses and would like to advertise in Ramciel Magazine, we have a variety of low-priced alternatives, which we will happily discuss with you. This will bring your businesses to the attention not only to the members of the Diaspora but also to our readers here. So, what will our next issues be covering? Along with our ongoing general coverage of South Sudanese events throughout the Diaspora,

we are open to any topic that reflects a credible issue, challenge, or accomplishment for our community. One question that indeed invites interest is mental health. We want to address that subject head-on, which will require the willingness of individuals to talk about their problems and treatments. Encouraging such honest communication is part of our role as we see it.

Ramciel will continue to stick to its mission statement by connecting the Diaspora and those back home in South Sudan and by educating our brothers and sisters in South Sudan about our life experiences in Diaspora. Of course, we also want Ramciel to entertain as well as enlighten.

We are committed to providing news of entertainers and people of interest and to promote the arts and entertainment efforts of both those who live in the Diaspora and those back home. In keeping with that goal of entertainment, Ramciel Magazine welcomes you and invites you to have a good time. Thank you so much!

SCOOP IT!

Where the News from the Diaspora and South Sudan Meet!

Chris Kartel Dem, Promoter/Activist

A twenty-three year old South Sudanese promoter based in Kampala, Uganda, Chris has been spreading a message of peace and community among South Sudanese artists in East Africa by uniting and teaching them how to love one another.

Betty Josheph

Betty Joseph is a South Sudanese student at Cairo University, Cairo Egypt. Studying Community Development.

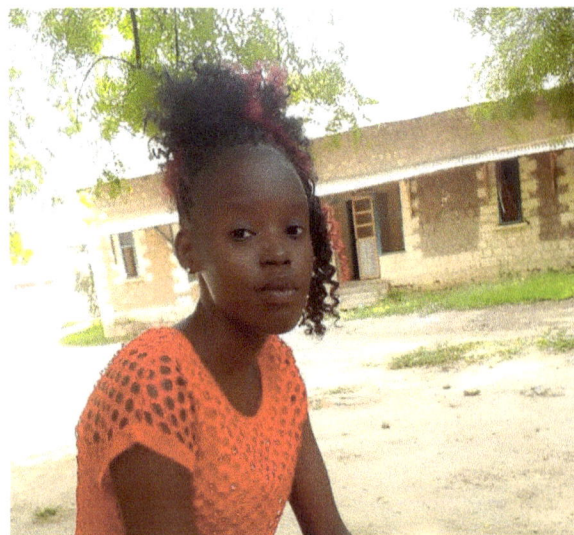

Athieng Santino Manyuat

Miss Manyuat is a twenty-one year old student at the University of Juba's College of Natural Resources and Environmental Studies. Her future ambition is to be an environmentalist and humanitarian.Her hobbies are reading, cooking, and making decorations, and her favorite movie is Let It Shine. She has recently read Life Without Tension and Strong Woman. Her fashion role model is Deepika Padukone from India.

SCOOP IT!

Where the News from the Diaspora and South Sudan Meet!

Silver -X- Saimoo, Musician

A superstar artist, he is one of the most recognized musicians in South Sudan. His most popular hits are Carolina, Jesus the Master, and Muwala. But it is not just his music that gets noticed. His unique dreadlock style is a different fashion on its own.

Reverend Anderia Arok Lual (In Red), Akol Akol, And Deng Deng from St. Paul the Apostle Sudanese Mission in Phoenix Arizona.

Amlyia Deng

Amlyia Deng, model, activist Miss Deng is a beautiful South Sudanese model and former first runner up of Miss World South Sudan 2018-2019. But it is not just the natural beauty that defines Miss Deng, she is a smart and intelligent activist who is currently working on several projects including an upcoming novel and a plan to build a library in South Sudan. She believes it will help deliver more than just intellectual information for our generations and generations to come.

SCOOP IT!

Where the News from the Diaspora and South Sudan Meet!

Bashir Jaythankz

Founder and CEO of Nyuonville Film Company, Mr. Jaythankz is an independent filmmaker based in Nairobi, Kenya. Nyuonville has produce over 70 skits, two short films and a feature film all of which are currently showing on YouTube Nyuonville TV channel. But enjoys traveling and swimming.

Adut Jennifer

Popularly known as Precious Dudu Majur, this banker loves reading and meeting new people.

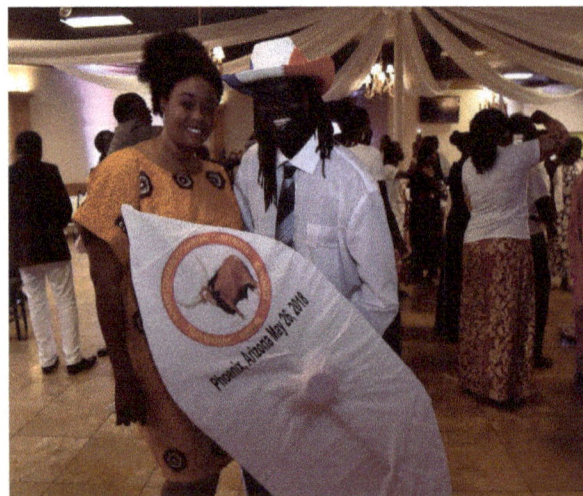

Dominic Deng

Comedian Dominic Deng a.k.a Deng Nyadeng and Ms. Ashai Arop Bagat during Adiang Mayom Fundraising in Phoenix

SCOOP IT!

Where the News from the Diaspora and South Sudan Meet!

Gordon Koang & Ms. Nyapal

Gordon Koang and Ms. Nyapal Lul are two amazing musical artists from South Sudan and proudly represent the best of our country.

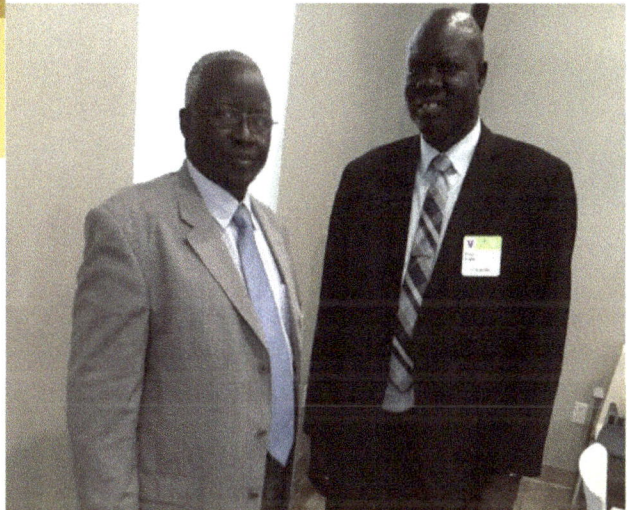

Mr. Kon Kueith & Hon. Atem Garang

Mr. Kon Kueith with Hon. Atem Garang during SSDA at USIP in Washington D.C.

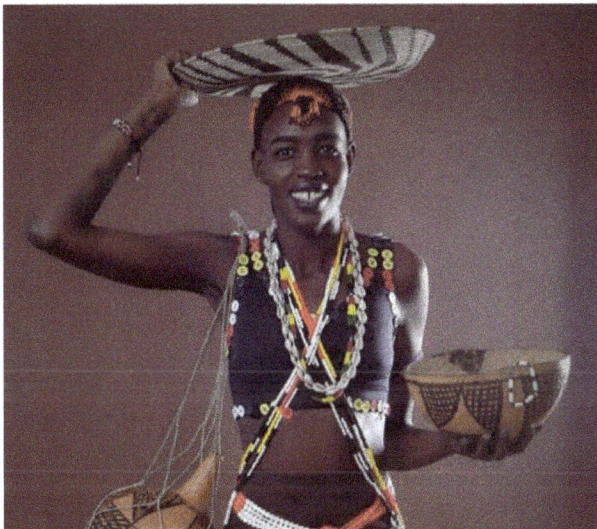

Jackline Achuei Deng Ajiing

A singer, actress, and model. Also known as Ting Tall Man, Miss Achuei Deng is an Afro-beat Singer, Actor, and fashion model, and a Youtube sensation. She has amassed a million views through her various Youtube videos.

SCOOP IT!

Where the News from the Diaspora and South Sudan Meet!

Hon. Awan Gol Riak & Dr. John Juba Malou

Hon. Awan Gol Riak and Dr. John Juba Malou in Phoenix, Arizona during Launching of Pion Nyan Abyei.

Mama Amira Ali & Mr. Yai Lyai

Mama Amira & Mr. Yai Lyai, chairman of Tonj Community Association in the U.S. during 2019 conference in Phoenix .

Ms. World South Sudan 2018 - Florence Thompson

Ms World South Sudan 2018 Florence Thompson with the Children at the Orphanage in Juba.

SCOOP IT!

Where the News from the Diaspora and South Sudan Meet!

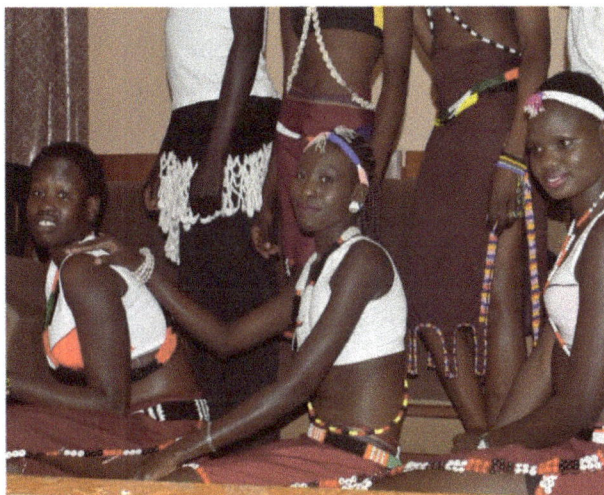

Twicmayardit Dance Group

Twicmayardit Dance Group

Twicmayardit Community Cultural Awareness in Nairobi 2018

Twicmayardit Dance Group

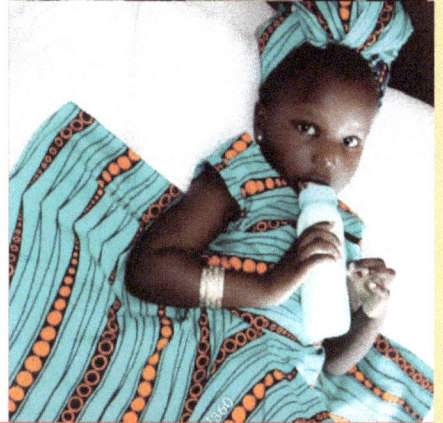

EKON360 ARLINGTON TEXAS

A U.S. base Private
Custom Design Africans Wears made with sophisticated, high quality Africans
fabrics from the finest materials available.
Like our page to receive
the latest trends and updates

Shop at www.ekon360.com

CHECK US OUT! ALWAYS SOMETHING NEW!

Treat yourself to a well-deserved shopping spree, and fill your
closet with great fashion finds!

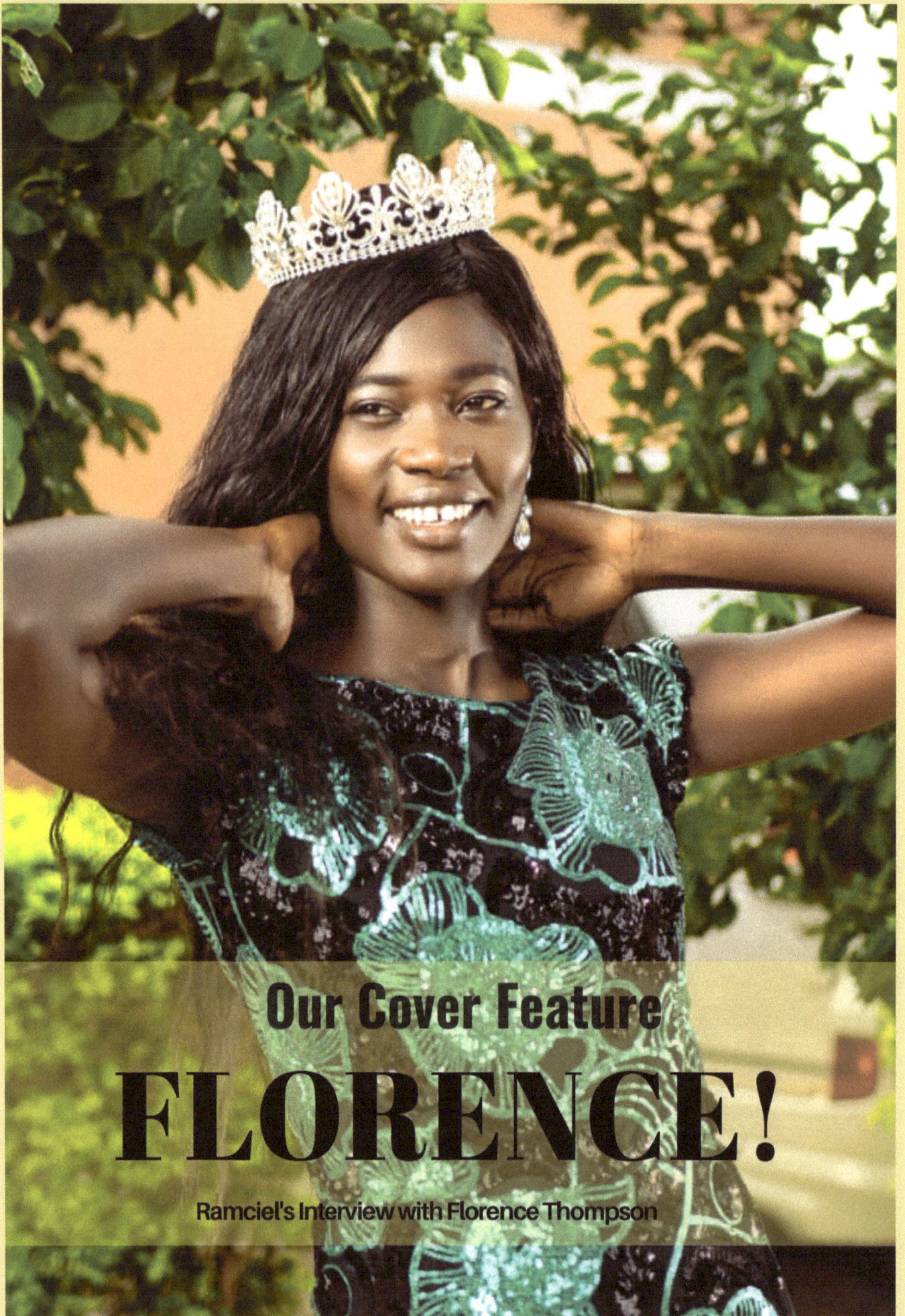

Our Cover Feature

FLORENCE!

Ramciel's Interview with Florence Thompson

This will be Ramciel Magazine's first interview with Former Miss World South Sudan after her reigns ended this year. Initial interview was conducted with Miss Thompson right away after she had emerged as the winner of Miss World South Sudan in October 14, 2018.

Ramciel Magazine: RM - Florence Thompson: FT

RM: What was it like taking part in the Miss World contest? **FT:** I was particularly excited to be asked to take part in the 2018 South Sudan Miss World pageant because I think many people think everything in South Sudan is about Dinka and about the conflicts between Dinka and Nuer. In reality our country is made up of many tribes, including my own the Lotoko. We are all one nation and I wanted to represent our country. We need to end tribalistic hinking and realize that we are all from this one amazing country. It was wonderful to win the pageant and go on to represent our wonderful country at the 68th Miss World competition in Sanya, China. I was proud to carry the culture and beauty of South Sudan around the world.

Coming in number 24 of the 128 competitors from around the world was a thrill. I only wish I had been selected a bit sooner so I could have prepared better. One of the best moments was carrying our South Sudanese flag and knowing that ours was the youngest country represented in the contest. Of course, taking part was not just about winning. Few people know much about our country. They thing of South Sudan as weak and underdeveloped. Many who approached me thought of our nation as poor and wracked by civil war. I got to tell them about our natural resources, our fertile land, our fascinating ecology, and our many wonderful regions and tribes. I told them they should come to visit our country and that they will be amazed by its beauty and diversity.

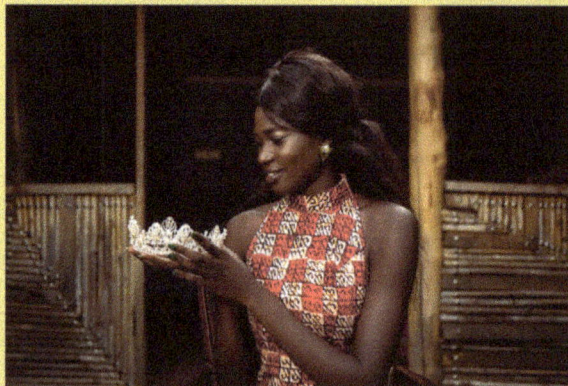

RM: Did you always want to be a beauty queen? **FT:** Actually, I grew up loving sports and was quite a tomboy. My father, who was my biggest fan encouraged me to take part in everything I wanted. He cheered me on whatever it was and especially told me how important it was to do well in school. Although we are from Torit in Eastern Equatoria, we lived in Juba, so there were wonderful opportunities. He gladly paid my school fees and paid for my sports uniforms. I was very lucky to have him as a dad. When I was 12, my father died. It was a terrible loss. I knew then that I would try to live my life in ways that would honor him. That was when I decided to become a doctor. I wanted to help other people live. I was fortunate that my stepmother was able to continue supporting my education. I was studying in Cairo when I was asked to take part in the contest. I took a leave from school so I could come back to South Sudan for the selection process. Of course, when I won, I had to let the school know that I would be extending the leave. First, there would be that wonderful trip to China and then my year of public appearances and representing our country.

RM: What have you enjoyed most about being the South Sudan Miss World and what has been the hardest part? **FT:** The best part. That's easy. I've been able to bring attention to our nation's children, especially to those who have been affected so cruelly by the civil conflicts. All children, no matter what their tribe or region, need and deserve good care and education. It breaks my heart to see children on the streets. I come from a loving, middle-class family, and I grew up wanting to help others. If I can raise awareness of the need and help direct resources to help those children, then this title will truly have meant something. The worst part? That, too, is easy. Interrupting my studies. At least, I have been able to spend more time with my family in Juba and to get to know other South Sudanese from all over our country.

RM: Do you think beauty contests are outdated or are they still relevant?   **FT:** I was astounded at how many people took part in the Miss World contest in Juba and how many people showed up to see it. It goes to show that people want something positive in their lives.   If the contest were simply about looks and had nothing to do with how we would use the resulting fame, I don't think it would be worthwhile.

The important thing is that anybody who achieves some fame if its from sports, beauty, academic achievements, business, politics: no matter what; they should try to o something with that fame to make the world a better place. Being South Sudan's Miss World has given me an opportunity to make a difference and I'm very thankful for the opportunity.

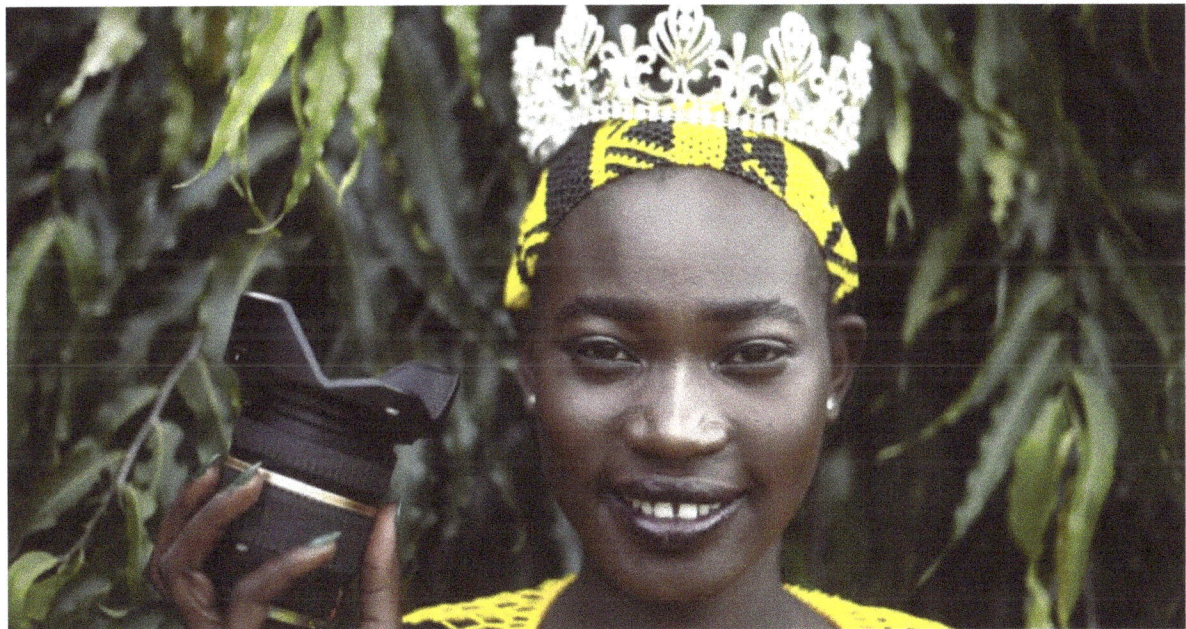

Advertise with Ramciel Magazine contact us at info@ramcielmagazine.com

BEST 100

Are you one of the Best Beautiful People in South Sudan or the Diaspora? Send us 3 of your best photos, your career or aspirations and your hobbies to info@ramcielmagazine.com to be featured on Ramciel Magazine Online. Here are 16 of the Best 100 Ladies of South Sudan and The Diaspora

Miss World South Sudan 2019 Mariah Nyayiena Joseph

BEST 100 OF SOUTH SUDAN

Former Miss Jonglei State - Jacky Mayen
Nyibol Bol
Zakira Luri
Sarah Gabriel
Athieng Santino

Submit Your Picture, Hobbies, Career, Location to
Ramciel Magazine's Best 100 Women.

See more at www.ramcielmagazine.com

BEST 100 OF SOUTH SUDAN

Amna Mami Millewa
Queen Zee Qz
Elena Bigoa Thon
Becky Abiem Akeen
Princess Abuk Akuol

Submit Your Picture, Hobbies, Career, Location to Ramciel Magazine's Best 100 Women.

See more at www.ramcielmagazine.com

"African Roots: Growing Food from Home in Australia

An Interview with Thuch Ajak of The United African Farm

The United Africa Farm in Australia.

Thank you for participating inour interview for Ramciel Magazine

Ramciel: What is the United African Farm?
Thuch Ajak: We are a community-based initiative in Melbourne, Australia, dedicated to growing food that matters for Australians who have come here from Africa.

Ramciel: What do you mean "food that matters?" Thuch Ajak: First, we want to grow crops that are commonly found in our homelands but are not readily available in the shops here in Australia, foods like okra, moloakia (Egyptian spinach), and cassava. Second, we want the food to matter to our members because they have been part of the growing process by volunteering to prepare the soil, sow, weed, and harvest. Even more importantly, these crops matter because we involve our children in the farm. We want our youth to learn how food is grown and we hope that some of them will go on to find employment in agriculture.

Ramciel: In a way this is like our homeland where the elders pass on traditional knowledge of farming and animal husbandry to the youth.

Thuch Ajak: Indeed; that has always been one of our goals. We want our children to understand that agriculture is a tool for economic, social, and political growth as well as a way to connect us one to another across regions, tribes, even nations. The soil is the mother of us all.

Ramciel: How did the United African Farm come into being? Thuch Ajak: I met Mama Queyea Tuazama, who came to Australia ten years ago from Liberia. We were attending a workshop on growing garlic. She told me about a piece of land she had acquired from a farmer. She and I invited a few friends to join us, and the United African Farm was born.

Ramciel: So from the beginning this was a pan-African project. Thuch Ajak: Yes. While at home we are so aware of diversity and the many cultures of our people, in the Diaspora we often think of ourselves as one tribe, one people. Within that sense of oneness, we still try to keep our individual cultures alive and pass an appreciation of them on to our children by holding festivals and celebrations. I see the United African Farm as a way to keep our traditions alive.

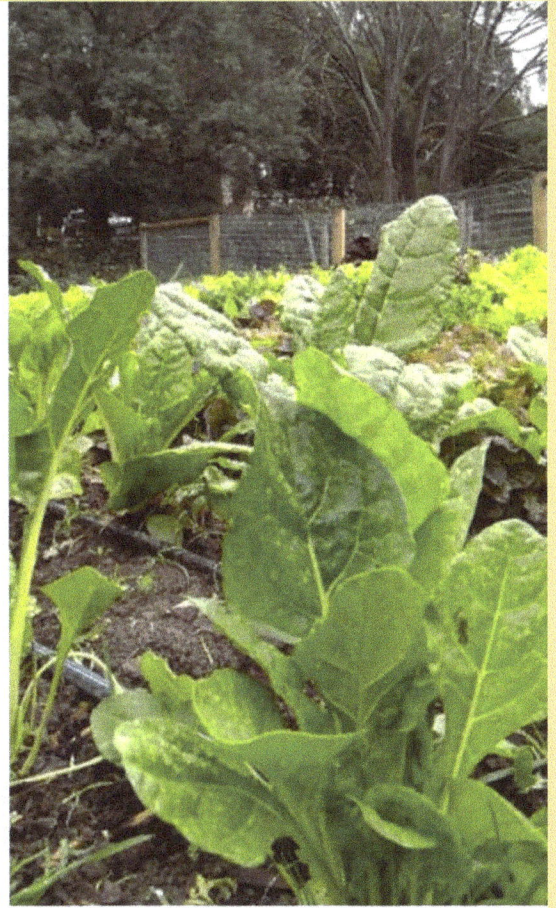

"We Teach The Importance of Farming!"

Ramciel: It sounds like you get great pleasure from your work with the farm? Thuch Ajak: My greatest joy is that the farm brings Africans together irrespective of their age, gender, religions, or cultures. It also gives us a way of growing our own food, expeciailly the delicacies we have missed from home.

Ramciel: What is the most difficult part of this project? Thuch Ajak: You might think that the farm work is the most difficult, especially since we do much of it using hand tools. However, the real job is getting people to turn up and volunteer. Sometimes, it feels like I spend all my time chasing after people.
Still, once they do get into the fields, see the crops, and get their hands in the soil, you can see the pleasure in their faces. At those moments, the work is well worth it.

Ramciel: Do you personally feel that connection to the crops and the soil? Thuch Ajak: Absolutely. I started farming as a refugee at Kakuma. We had fields around the borehole zone near Kakuma 2. That was when I was in primary school. Later on, I pursued a degree in agriculture at the University of Upper Nile. That was in 2013. For me, agriculture is fun. It is also life. The art and science of caring for the land, crops and animals is the noblest thing that humans should do to Mama Earth. I feel blessed and happy to have taken this journey.

Ramciel: Is the African Farm sustainable? Will it continue over the years? Thuch Ajak: That's the plan. We are producing crops which can be sold to pay workers, offer volunteers some incentives, and buy tools. Our long-term vision is creating a cultural space for our kids and everyone, somewhere you can find African food, culture, and unity. There is a lot to do, but I think we can make it work. Right now, most of the work is done by volunteers. We go out and beat the drums to get community mobilization. Currently, there are two paid positions at the farm and we are seeking grants to help us grow.

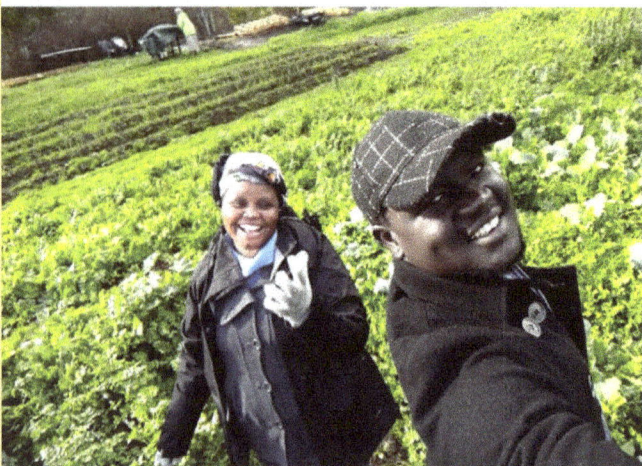

Ramciel: Do you have livestock on the farm? Thuch Ajak: Not yet. Of course, raising animals is a big thing in many African cultures, and someday we hope to have those animals here. Our first livestock will be beehives. We hope to train some young apiculturists and possibly to produce some honey for our community. But for now, we only have vegetables.

Ramciel: This is an "African" venture; are there other groups or nationalities that do communal farming here in Australia? Thuch Ajak: Yes, there are other community gardens. What makes us unique is that we have members from ten African countries.

Ramciel: Are you receiving outside support? Thuch Ajak: Many individuals and organizations have been helping us. Many farmers have opened their land to us so that we can see how they are doing things and some have donated tools to our organization. Currently, we are lobbying for government support.

Ramciel: Does the fact that the African Farm is in Australia rather than in Africa create any challenges. Thuch Ajak: The climate is different. Of course, Africa is a huge continent with many climate zones, but for me, I come from a far more tropical climate than we have in Melbourne. That means that we have only a small growing window for crops that in Africa may be planted more than once in a year. Also, climate change is affecting us. Drought is common here in Australia, and that means we have to adapt. One of our challenges is to teach the children not only how we used to grow things in our homelands but how to adapt to the changing world.

Ramciel: Thanks for taking part in this interview. Is there anything else you would like to say in closing, perhaps something to people in other areas who might wish to start a project like the United African Farm? Thuch Ajak: As you know, most Africans come from an agricultural background. When we come to the Western World we often lose that connections to farming. We don't have access to land and we don't teach our children to value the soil. There is always a connection between the soil and humans; it is therapeutic to maintain that connection. Not only is farming about growing healthy food but it is also about nurturing our souls and our mental health.

CONTINUING THE LEGACY!

By Nybol Madut Bol

I woke up to exciting news, my little nephew Bol Manute Bol was being drafted into the NBA. Tears of joy rolled down my cheeks as I woke my infant daughter for her breakfast. Her fingers traced the drops along my face.

When we lost our brother, Manute Bol, it had torn my heart apart. Nothing will ever bring him back. But looking at his children, I knew that one of them would continue their father's legacy. When, on June 20th, Bol Manute was picked for the Denver Nuggets—just one day after the anniversary of his father's death in 2010—it was a time for rejoicing.

Thank you, God, for being with the entire Bol family and especially Manute's mom all these difficult years. We are thankful that my brother's name is alive and his place in professional basketball remembered. I wish he were here to witness his son's being drafted into the NBA

Bol, know that all your family, friends, and the entire nation of South Sudan are proud of you. We take pride in your accomplishments and support you all the way. As I think back to my own younger days when I, too, played basketball, I wish you many great games to come.

INTERVIEW WITH FORMER VICE-PRESIDENT OF THE REPUBLIC OF SUDAN, GEN. GEORGE KONGOR AROP

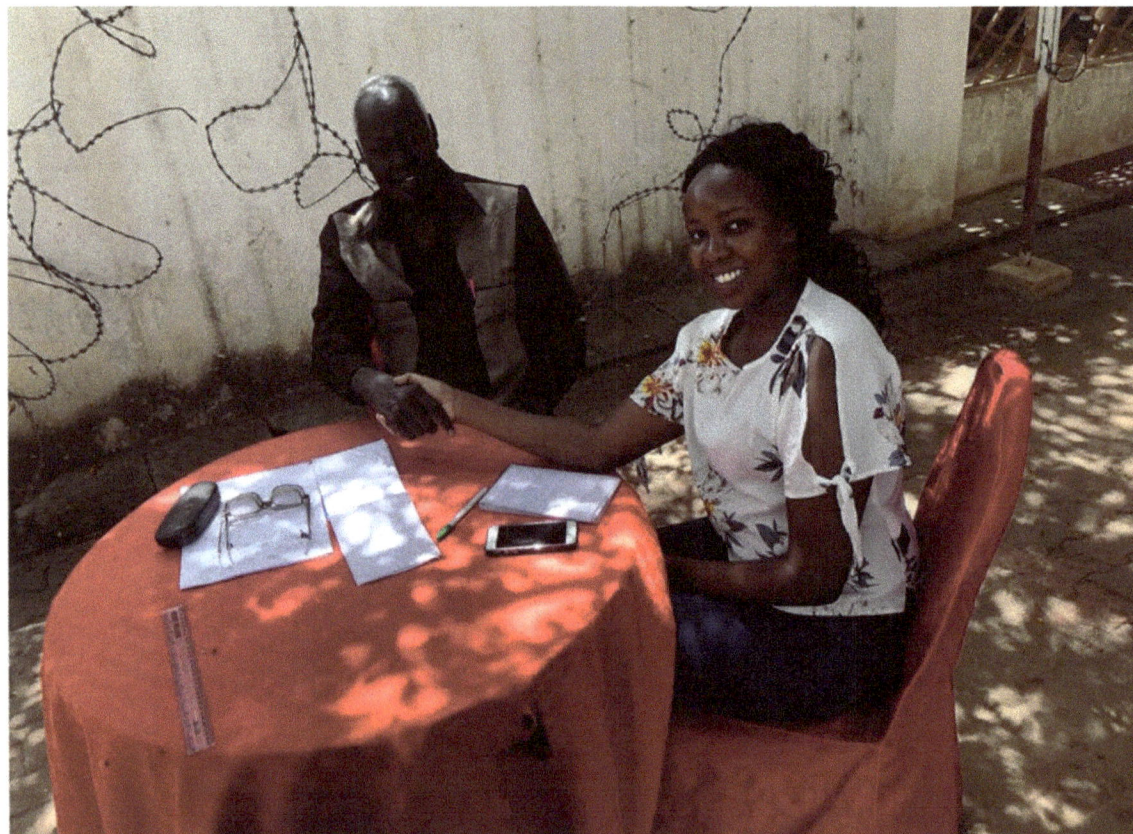

George Kongor Arop, was born in 1947 in Kongor, Tonj. He attended Tonj Intermediate School and Rumbek Secondary School. In 1971 he graduated from police college. As a police officer, he was posted throughout the country, to towns such as Medani, Kosti, Wau, Juba and Renk. From 1991 to 1994 he was the governor of Bahr el Ghazal, and from 1994 to 2000 he was the second Vice President of Sudan. 2001 to 2004 he was a member of the assembly in Khartoum. In 2006 he became President of the African National Congress.

By Adhieu Majok

Adhieu: Thank you so much for your time to take this interview for the second edition of Ramciel Magazine. I will be asking about your past position as second Vice President, your position in the African National Congress party, and your thoughts about politics in general.

As second Vice President, did you feel the position was ceremonial given the current circumstances at the time, or did you believe you had the opportunity to make decisions and affect change for South Sudan?

Gen. George: I was appointed as second Vice President and this position was always allotted to by Southerners. It was not ceremonial. You have to get into the system of the presidency, and when I was appointed, there were many challenges. There was war in the country, and most of the people were displaced. The social fabric of the Southerners was broken because they were displaced from the environment where they were raised, and they faced many difficulties.

I had to see to it that the Southerners who went to the north of the country had a conducive atmosphere created for them. I had to work day and night to see that they had lodging, that they could live peacefully and get what they needed from me or the government. I had to supervise the security, too. As Vice President I responded when from time to time there were problems of local drinks, people being harassed, and ladies being taken to prisons. Still, we intervened and, although we did not stamp it out completely, we had to reduce it.

Education of their children was one of the first things I faced as well. I had to make what I would call 'displaced schools' for them near their lodging. This was not a handout from our brothers in the north. It was real work.

Two, when they [students] reached the level of universities, I had to create what is called special intake because our children were not competing.

Adhieu: They were not competing? Gen. George: Well they were not competing because they'd usually get very low percentages and as such, we had to create a special intake process. They were being cheated in the areas of medicine, engineering and many others. So I convinced my colleagues in the presidency and made a decision that was welcomed. We managed to graduate almost over 5000 of those special intake students. Those who you see in the offices here, they did not come from East Africa, America or London. So if we were a décor, we wouldn't have educated our people, we wouldn't have protected our people.

We helped them cross the river to the other side, with very minimum casualties. We were not a décor. We managed. If we were a décor or whatever people think about us, we wouldn't have managed to bring peace, which we are now enjoying. It was our pressure in the National Congress Party where we pushed what we wanted. Every time when we met with people, when they brought to us proposals or initiatives from other areas, we usually told them the initiatives fell short of self-determination and that the people of the South would not accept those initiatives.

Adhieu: You mean self-determination in terms of the country? Gen. George: Yes, self determination. Self-determination means you decide on your fate. Either you become independent as we have now achieved, or you have to make unity with your choice, but not the choice of other people.

So this is where we succeeded. That's why we inside, and people outside, were having one intention and one name. It was very clear that was the only way out for Southerners, and that is ultimately what Southerners unanimously agreed upon.

Also when I was Vice President, I was responsible for the Southern Desk. I was checking on how we could really develop the South. I can assure you that we did much. It was on this base which we laid, in education, in security, in politics, where we now have the peace we are forging. If we were just a décor, as people may say, there wouldn't have been peace. However, all of us were on one wavelength, and that is why I believe that we maintained the social fabric until we achieved what we have now.

Adhieu: That is a really good answer, because you have shown that the position you had was not just for the name, but you had work to do, you had to manage the South. You had the chance to make major changes that our country is based on now. On that same note, what were some of the biggest challenges that you faced in this role?

Gen. George: Well, there were a lot of challenges. Challenge one, Southerners thought that whoever was in the government was fighting your people, they may think you were just a nut which can be screwed and put on just like any other. We made it very clear we are not nuts, we are politicians, we are personalities. When we have a problem we have to be realistic in all that we do. Most of the people, at the end of the day, found that we were really doing a proper job. And sister, to be in a government which is fighting your people is not an easy thing, and a person who is there is not a simple person.

We managed to cross our people to peace with minimal casualties. If you compare what we have now, how many losses we have, and the losses we had the other day before the independence, you will find there is a very big gap. That was one of the challenges. Southerners did not want to accept any Southerner to be in the government that was fighting people in the South. But we made it very clear, there's a lot to be helped if you're in the government. At the end of the day, they believed in us, that there was a need.

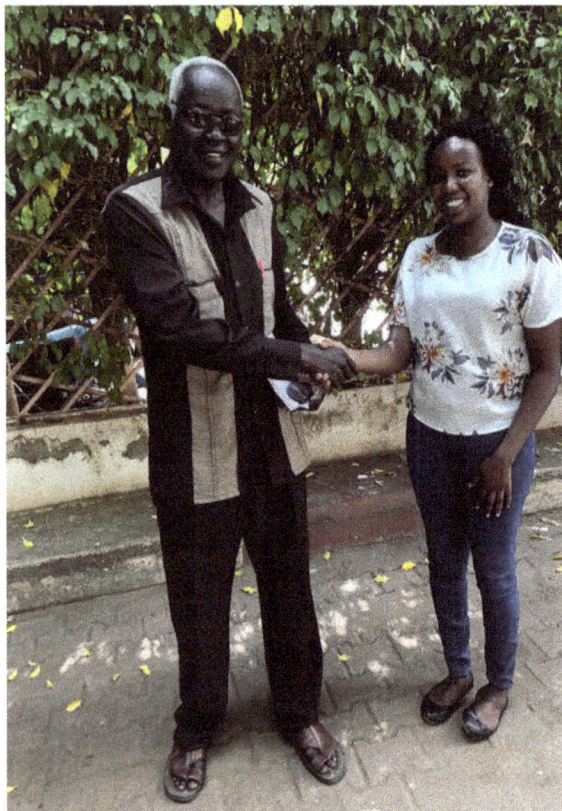

Adhieu: So you mean that politicians fighting the Northern government were in the Northern government? Gen. George: There was war in the country and Southerners believed that you cannot be in a government that is fighting your people. Northerners think that all Southerners are the same, whether they are in the government or not. It was a big challenge. But it had to be done. We swallowed the bitter pains and continued with the journey. Here we are.

Adhieu: There was a lot of criticism. What was your view on the Southern movement, the SPLM/A?
Gen. George: When this war started, it did not start out of nowhere. It was a decision of Southerners who met and said, "We have been talking with the North, and the North holds out the positions of change. The only way is to fight." It was a decision made by Southerners, whether you were in or outside, it was a decision. Some took arms, others provided food. Others took the role of giving information on how to fight the war. So there was a division of roles.

Those who decided to go and fight, is equally the same as the person who decided to give you food or information on how to fight the war. So we usually asked ourselves, everybody had a role. If you went and died in the field, you died for the cause of the South. If you were arrested, and then you were slaughtered because you were giving food to an enemy or giving information, you have died for the cause of the South. So Southerners were doing one thing inside and outside in the diaspora, they were doing one thing. I do not believe that anybody is more equal than others, everybody is the same. If someone considers that only the one who held a gun did much, then that is unfortunate.

So when the referendum came, 98% Southerners voted for independence. This shows that whether you were a farmer or brewing already for your child to go to school so he or she could become a doctor or an engineer, we also consider him a liberator.

So, we have now gained our independence. It was just our white paper, which brought it. We should see clearly that everyone in the South did his job, whether in the diaspora or inside the country, or fighting, all of us, did a good job.

Adhieu: I appreciate that, because I was born in the diaspora, and my parents also played their role there. My next question is, can you tell me a little bit about the creation of Warrap State, because I know you were once the governor of Bahr el Ghazal, and then Warrap was created while you were Vice President? Gen. George: Well, no. In 1991, I became a governor of Greater Bahr el Ghazal. I went at a time when the social fabric was completely destroyed. The town (Wau) was divided into three zones; one for Dinka, one for Jur, one for Fertit. People were butchering themselves. I went when things were critical. Because I was going to an area where I knew people, I knew the composition in the society, so I held a lot of talks. Because of the movement outside, Dinka were considered sympathisers of SPLM without exception. The other side, the Fertit, they were considered loyal to the government. So when I went, I got these three groups. I met with the Dinka elders, and the first question they asked me was, "How did you come here? When a governor comes here, he must work according to what we say." My simple answer was, "I am a government, and no citizen can ask akuma, what is he doing? The government only consults them and gives them the program."

The Fertit also came, they told me, "George, you are not a governor." "What am I?" "You're a Dinka, you're a Dinka governor." "Why, because I am a Dinka?" "This is how we are seeing you." Adhieu, I told them, "By day I am a governor, by night I am a governor, I will give you the program." I gave them the program. The program, how I brought peace to Wau, was first of all, I had the confidence. I enjoyed the confidence of the people because I had been a police officer there, and I treated all the population with equality. So I enjoyed their support. I began with a women's conference and simply they denied all the insecurity and hatred happening among all the groups, and they came out to support me. When a lady supports you, your information goes very fast.

So, my message was that I needed unity and security. I needed people to abandon the way they were thinking so automatically, this message reached those who were fighting because they were the mothers of the youth who were fighting. They were the wives of the elders who were complicating things. So the message came out very quickly and very clearly. The next was the youth, who were being used. I had a conference for them, and they also gave me their support to bring peace, development and social cohesion among the tribes. They also denied those elders who were messing up their security.

I gave them a program. Their program, which is almost 16 hours, they only sleep 8 hours, and we work for 16 hours. There was no room for drunkenness, idleness, playing dominos and many other things. Every weekend, I came and gave them a lecture. I said every weekend on Saturday we must have a rally, and in this rally, everybody must speak out because I know what they usually say in your fences, so I came and cleared all those doubts which people are talking about and cleared them. Wau became peaceful. People became united. When people were divided, coming to your point, people decided to decentralise the Sudan into different states. Myself, I was against it.

Adhieu: The creation of ten states? Gen. George: I was against the redivision of Southern Sudan. I made it very clear that I was not for it because of the reasons I stated.

Adhieu: Because it divides people? Gen. George: It divides people on ethnicity and when you are divided as a tribe, people will go after you, and if your neck is very stiff, they break it. I did not want that way of redivision of the South. With this, my resistance, well they managed to divide the South into nine states. After I learned they divided it into nine states, and they were about to declare, what is called now Warrap, people of Toni were taken to Rumbek.

People of Gogrial were taken to Aweil. So it became my concern. Gogrial was a sub-district of Tonj. The division that was made, you find a big district is amalgamated, with sub-districts. Rumbek and Yirol. Raja and Wau. Why do that? By that time I was relieved because you cannot control a big region, and when it is divided into three, you cannot become a governor of three states. It took us a hell of a long time with my brothers like Ali Osman, Al-Bashir, I was asking them, "Did I not perform well or what? Because my people are being divided. If I performed well, then my people cannot be dispersed.

Some going to Aweil, and they have no connection with Aweil." I found that I was being punished, my people are being punished for something they did not do. At the end of the day, they said, "George, we have again amalgamated Gogrial and Tonj to be one state. What do you say about it?" I was not a selfish politician, I will not take the state to Tonj, it would look very absurd because I was the one who was governor, and if I take it to my own area, it would not be wanted by the people. So I decided, let us take it to Warrap, because Warrap is equidistant.

Adhieu: Is Warrap Town in Tonj? Gen. George: Yes. Warrap has history, that's where all the chiefs were appointed by the British. It is also equidistant, when you go to the area of Madien Anyuon, it is almost 100 miles. If you go to Tongliep, it is almost 70 miles. If you go to Mayen Juur, the end of Gogrial district, it is almost 60 or 70 miles, so I got it. This is the history of how we created Warrap. So it was really shameful when people of Tonj made an agreement with people of Gogrial, to give them the capital, and we get the governorship. It was really a mockery. You cannot sell your land because of positions.

Adhieu: That is what happened, because now it is still called Warrap state, and we still did not have the capital or the governor? Gen. George: Yes, Anei Kueindit became the governor and Warrap was taken to Kuajok. It was really shameful. Later on, Anei was dismissed, he did not even spend a year. Then Bol Madut came, he also did not spend a year. After that, they lost the promise.

Adhieu: Only now when we got our own state, we managed to do something to some degree. We will come onto that later. This is a very direct question; do you have any ambition for the highest office or are you thinking of standing for elections after the transitional period? Gen. George: *laughs* It is too early to talk about it and it is not my decision.

Adhieu: It is not your decision, it is your people's decision, if they want you to go you will go. Are you currently a political participant or an observer? Do you feel you are actively participating in the politics of South Sudan?

Adhieu: Is Warrap Town in Tonj? Gen. George: Yes. Warrap has history, that's where all the chiefs were appointed by the British. It is also equidistant, when you go to the area of Madien Anyuon, it is almost 100 miles. If you go to Tongliep, it is almost 70 miles. If you go to Mayen Juur, the end of Gogrial district, it is almost 60 or 70 miles, so I got it. This is the history of how we created Warrap. So it was really shameful when people of Tonj made an agreement with people of Gogrial, to give them the capital, and we get the governorship. It was really a mockery. You cannot sell your land because of positions.

Adhieu: That is what happened, because now it is still called Warrap state, and we still did not have the capital or the governor? Gen. George: Yes, Anei Kueindit became the governor and Warrap was taken to Kuajok. It was really shameful. Later on, Anei was dismissed, he did not even spend a year. Then Bol Madut came, he also did not spend a year. After that, they lost the promise.

Adhieu: Only now when we got our own state, we managed to do something to some degree. We will come onto that later. This is a very direct question; do you have any ambition for the highest office or are you thinking of standing for elections after the transitional period? Gen. George: *laughs* It is too early to talk about it and it is not my decision.

Adhieu: It is not your decision, it is your people's decision, if they want you to go you will go. Are you currently a political participant or an observer? Do you feel you are actively participating in the politics of South Sudan? Gen. George: Yes, ANC is very active. We are not doing petty politics which are connected with positions or tribal affiliations, no. It is the African National Congress which is dealing with national issues that affect the nation. These are the issues we are dealing with. Today, we will not blow trumpets but we will have to say that we exist in the schools, we exist in the universities, in the streets, we are everywhere. We deal with national issues such as peace, security, the economy of the country which is crumbling... these are the basics we are all interested in.

Adhieu: So basically you would say those are some of the objectives of the ANC? Gen. George: Yes, we have our platform and we will give you our platform. The ANC platform are the policies of the party.

Adhieu: What do you want to achieve with the ANC and what legacy do you want to leave with the ANC? Gen. George: The legacy is what you do and what you leave behind. When you form a party, you don't form a party because you want to. As I told you, there are objectives which are there, and these objectives will bring the legacy. In the ANC, we want to leave highly informed cadres. We have a slogan – we see, we feel, we reach. When we are seeing our people suffering, we feel ashamed because we are the leaders of these people, and as such, we must work hard. When we are feeling, we are feeling responsible for our people. If you are responsible for these people, you are not doing much for them. So what do you do? You have to double your efforts to reach them. How do you reach their hearts? You reach their hearts by doing a noble job for them. So our slogan is, we see, we feel, we reach. When we have reached their hearts, we tell them that the ANC is the real choice.

If you are responsible for these people, you are not doing much for them. So what do you do? You have to double your efforts to reach them. How do you reach their hearts? You reach their hearts by doing a noble job for them. So our slogan is, we see, we feel, we reach. When we have reached their hearts, we tell them that the ANC is the real choice.

Adhieu: That is a really good promotion. Gen. George: It is the real choice. Two, when we feel that we have reached the hearts of the people and we are the real choice, and we get what we want, we must really leave something behind, we as individuals, we as leaders, when we go, we have to be remembered.

Adhieu: Now I will remember the ANC. Gen. George: Aiwa, it is the real choice.

Adhieu: I will ask you more about the ANC, outside of this interview. Now these are just some follow up questions. Could you explain the difference in politics, during your time when you were very active, compared to today's politics? How does it differ? Gen. George: There is a big difference. The country has been divided into 32 states.

Adhieu: You didn't agree with ten states, so 32 must be worse? Gen. George: It is worse because by that time there were resources. With 32 states, there are no resources. You find someone sitting under a tree, he calls himself an office. He has no office.

Adhieu: Under the tree commissioner? Gen. George: And he has nothing to deliver. Also you go and find the government of the governor, of the state, walking on foot, no cars, no accommodation, no what. During our times, a minister has an office, a governor has an office. He has a budget, he has to deliver services to the people. Now, there is nothing. It is power. What is power if you cannot give services to the people? It is meaningless. I only believe in what is called local government. It is only the local government which can develop us. We need devolution of powers to the local government, and when federal arrangements come, they will rest on a concrete local government.

But now people are calling for federalism, but where are the cadres? Where are the spirit people? Who can do the job? You cannot be taught on the job. You are sacrificing people because of power. Now, tribalism has come up very seriously because of positions and this federal or decentralization arrangement which has been done. Federal, or a decentralized system, does not mean you, as a son of that place, will be the only person who can deliver services to the people. Any person coming from any area can deliver services to the people, and they will not be involved in the petty politics of the area. Empowerment of the people to have their own administration does not mean that you are the person to deliver. This has been misunderstood by our people and people continue to misunderstand it until we reach a dark tunnel, and that dark tunnel is coming.

Adhieu: My question on that line is, I think you noticed also that the quality of our politicians has changed. Some examples are those becoming commissioners without any prior experience. What are your suggestions of how this country can be run or managed? Gen. George: The political appetite is so sharp. It is sharpening properly, and that is why a primary school leaver, can say "I want to become a commissioner, I want to become a governor, I want to become a minister." And that is why things are falling apart because of the inexperienced are creating more politicians in a country where resources are not yet tapped properly. When you come into office, you just get relieved. Where do you go? Ma indak, you don't have. You don't have a profession where you can go and live on. So you will still like to come back and fight, so that you become a politician. We have created a lot of politicians who are half-baked. That is our problem now. If you go to Tonj, your own state now, you have a lot of politicians.

If you ask them, what have you done in the position which you are in? He cannot tell you because now, positions have been made so that you do things for yourself, and not to serve the people. This is what is happening. I am completely dismayed and I am completely against the creation of politicians who are outside of the parameters of parties. What are called the communities, they are taking up the work of political parties, and it becomes really dangerous.

Adhieu: Is it community politics that become personality politics?   Gen. George: Yes, which is very dangerous. Politics must be through political parties. Communities are only for development and other social problems in a given social group or community. Sometimes, they come and say, we are nominating this man to go, from where? What do you know about this man? He is not a party cadre. How do you nominate him? So our politics are in mess.

Adhieu: So the only way for this country to be managed is to get out of this kind of politics?   Gen. George: Yes, we have to get into political parties. The only way forward is for the political parties to bring in their cadres, according to their knowledge. But if you go and you choose randomly, in a community, that is where things fall apart, and that is why we are not making headway.

Adhieu: Exactly. On that note, what advice would you give the politicians of this country and also the youth?   Gen. George: My advice is that we have gained our independence and the country which we fought for, for which we have lost lives and property. It would be ideal if all of us agreed on what I call national issues, which can promote existence in our country. Yes, there is where you come from, you may come from a community, you may come from a tribe, but a tribe cannot make you a leader and a community cannot make you a politician. You cannot come and ask for a position which brings people together when you are coming as a tribal politician. Everybody is entrenched in their tribe, which is endangering South Sudan. As leaders we have to come out in a very big way to denounce tribalism. We are not denouncing tribe, but we are denouncing tribalism. Whoever wants to be a leader needs to denounce tribalism.

Two, getting power should not be through violence. We should consider our people who fought all along with us, using their property, their children. We have to respect them. We have to respect their will. They are the only people who own power and we must adhere to their will. Grabbing power through communal violence, or tribal violence, or because of your tribe needs to be denounced properly. Let us be people of the South, talking one language and one voice. Then we will have no problem.

 Adhieu: Do you feel there was more unity during the time before independence?   Gen. George: I cannot tell you that there was a real unity among Southerners, because also the enemy was using some of the Southern tribes, dividing them. We Southerners we have to make a 180 degree turn. We cannot practice what was practiced by our former rulers, our brothers in the North. If we do, we have not liberated ourselves.

Adhieu: Do you feel there was more unity during the time before independence? Gen. George: I cannot tell you that there was a real unity among Southerners, because also the enemy was using some of the Southern tribes, dividing them. We Southerners we have to make a 180 degree turn. We cannot practice what was practiced by our former rulers, our brothers in the North. If we do, we have not liberated ourselves.

Adhieu: I have one last question, it goes all the way back again. So you were a member of the National Congress Party. What years were you a member and also what role did you play in that party? Gen. George: Yes, I was a member of the NCP. In the NCP, we had what is called the Southern Forum. That Southern Forum within the NCP was to deal with things which were exclusively to do with the South.

Adhieu: Would you say that the self determination cause was on the table? Gen. George: Yes, we also discussed it. Whenever there was a problem, we used to sit as a Southern Forum.

Adhieu: That is really amazing, I never knew a lot of these things. So when people read this interview, they will be very amazed. A lot of people are trying to link those who worked in the North, as those who had no intention of self-determination. Gen. George: That is absolutely, what can I say, nonsense or irrelevant? In the beginning of the interview, I said all of us, when this movement started people sat and divided the roles. If you don't know the role which was assigned to X or Y, then you do not know why you were fighting.

Adhieu: That is true. The war had to be fought on all fronts.

Gen. George: Yes, and so the roles were divided. We came out peacefully, with minimal loss. If we all had gone to the movement , what would have become of us? We had to be with these people and we managed to push through all that we could to help stabilize our people.

Adhieu: My final question now is because of what has happened in Sudan recently, do you think it will have an impact on the current peace process, particularly because Al-Bashir was brokering the peace agreement with Museveni in September last year? What do you think is the future of this country in terms of peace and security? Gen. George: This is a good question. Well, Bashir, did a lot. He was the first Northerner to recognize that Southerners have a problem. All Northern politicians used to say the problem of the South is just a storm in a tea cup. But when Bashir came, with his bravery, well he decided to fight, but when he found that it was not peaceful, he had to make another move. I was the first person to take the letter to Baba Ginda in 1988. The first meeting of the SPLM, with the government, I was the one who initiated it. I went to Nigeria twice, to bring the letter to Baba Ginda. He was the president at the time, he welcomed it, that there should be a dialogue in Nigeria, Abuja I and Abuja II. He continued to push all the peace dialogues until he said, "I will be the first man to give my congratulations if you South succeed!"

Which he actually did! When the South got independence, he was the first person to recognize South Sudan as an independent country. Two, although he [Bashir] did these things because of his own problems at home, still it is commendable that he did his best and this relative peace that we are enjoying now is through Bashir. Those who are now in Khartoum, one of their slogans is that Omar Al-Bashir separated the South. We will not go back until South comes back.

Adhieu: Oh, I think I have seen that one. The women were protesting and chanting. Gen. George: You saw it? Yes. So we Southerners also, we are observing critically, what will those who were holding out, and sloganeering that the South must come back, will it really be the voice of the government? So, with the going of Bashir. Well, we have nothing to say about it, it is the choice of the people. But I am happy that the government came out with a statement that they are going to honour all agreements. So we hope that this agreement is one of the agreements that is being honoured. So for us, we are observing what the next step by the government of South Sudan is.

Adhieu: Isn't the ANC under the Other Political Parties? Gen. George: Yes, we are OPP in the agreement. The ANC is a signatory to the agreement and that is why we are really pushing hard. Some people think that there are certain areas or clauses within the agreement which can be maneuvered, but we say an agreement is an agreement. We as the ANC are with the agreement, in spirit and letter. No way out because we believe this is the last chance for us and everyone must understand that. Either we remain as the South, or we go into fragmentation.

Adhieu: I'm very happy with this interview. I think you have covered so much maybe there is more that you would like to add? Gen. George: I am happy that Ramciel Magazine has traveled a long way to come and interview Southern leaders. We hope that this is not the the last interview with us. We all hope that you will come back from time to time, to conduct interviews, to know the positions of leaders in South Sudan. The magazine should encourage you to talk on politics, on economy, and on social issues of this country.

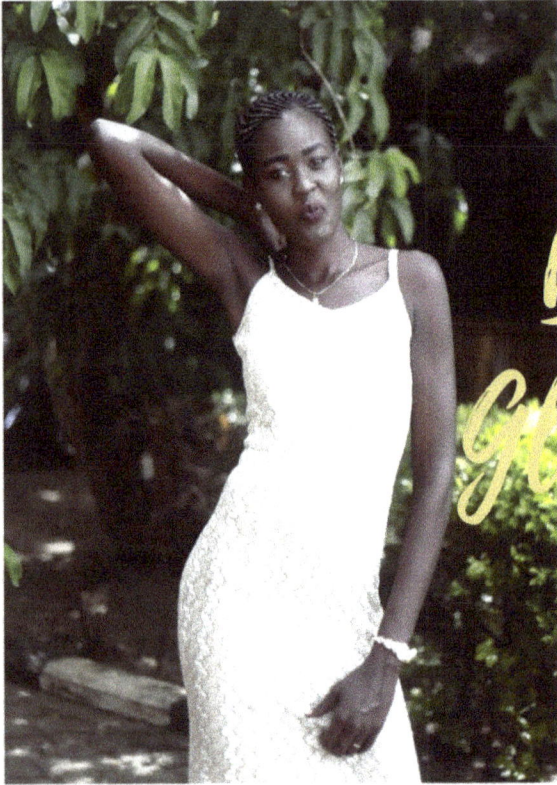

Becoming a Global Model

"I enjoy talking to crowds and seeing their expressions..."

Suzan Nyidier Makor

A beautiful twenty-one year-old South Sudanese model and college student at the Starford International University in Juba. Her hobbies include modeling, dancing, reading novels, watching movies, and playing volleyball and cricket. She enjoys talking to crowds and loves seeing the audience's expression listening to her, especially when leading and representing others in a group. Currently, she is a model within South Sudan, but is looking forward to becoming a global model from South Sudan.

As a model, her advice to young South Sudanese girls is that if modeling is what you love and desire, then do it. "I love modeling. If that is what you love and desire, then do it." To parents who might have reservations about their children become models or entering other careers in which they will be attracting attention, she says, "Allowing your child to do what they love is real caring." She adds, "Modeling, acting, dancing, and all forms of sport help build confidence and motivation. We need the young people of South Sudan to develop their will to succeed." Miss Makor wants to become an entrepreneur and to use that company to help build an orphanage for those who need a place to call home.

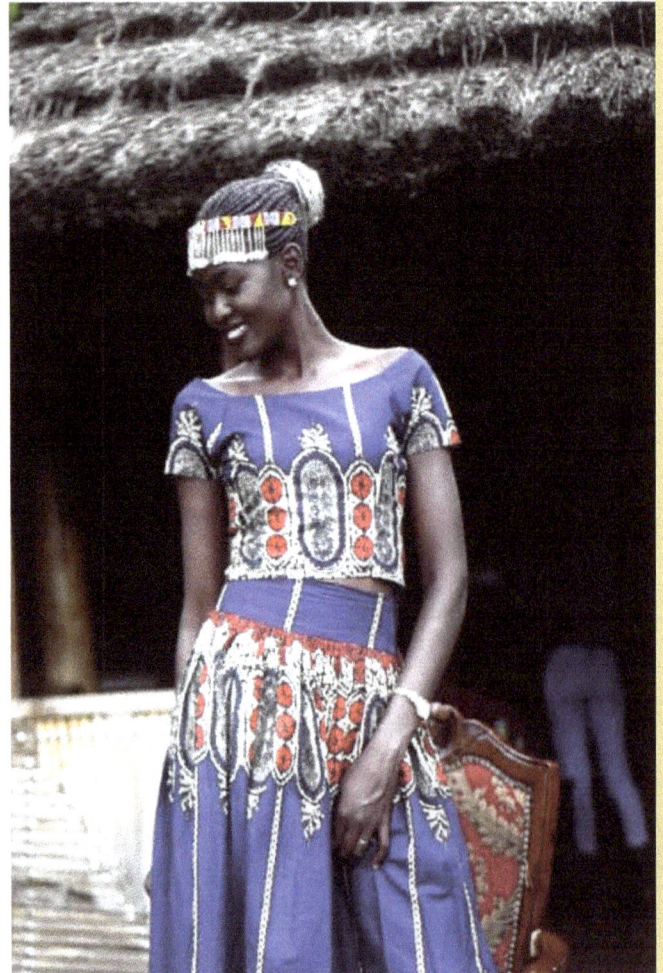

BEST 100

Are you one of the Best Beautiful People in South Sudan or the Diaspora? Send us 3 of your best photos, your career or aspirations and your hobbies to info@ramcielmagazine.com to be featured on Ramciel Magazine Online. Here are 16 of the Best 100 Men of South Sudan and The Diaspora.

Emmanuel Jal

BEST 100 OF SOUTH SUDAN

Changekouth Nyantungomg
Gatnyamiraan
Valentino Achak Deng
Deng Majok Chol
Atem Anyuom
Thiik Ajak Deng

Submit Your Picture, Hobbies, Career, Location to Ramciel Magazine's Best 100 Men.

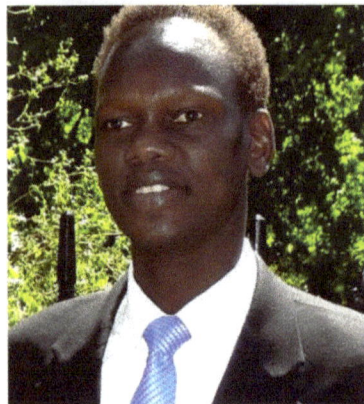

See more at www.ramcielmagazine.com

BEST 100 OF SOUTH SUDAN

Michael Kutey
Makuach Ayuel
Maal Maker Thiong
Machar A Deng
Madit D. Ring Yel

Submit Your Picture, Hobbies, Career, Location to Ramciel Magazine's Best 100 Men.

See more at www.ramcielmagazine.com

YAR MANYANG KHANG

Makuach Payam, Jonglei

A finalist pursuing her Bachelor's Degree in Business Management with a specialization in finance and banking at Moi University in Kenya. She also works with the Nile Sustainable Development Organization in South Sudan.

When she has free time, Miss Khang is a model. Willing to travel and to push her schedule, she has been rewarded by landing some photo advertisements.

If she could make one thing better in this world it would be that every child should have a home. "No child should be in the road, but some find themselves there. Not by choice or fault but unavoidable circumstances." It is her belief that every child has a right to healthy living and education. "Street children receive neither and that is not how it should be."

"BEING IN THE COMPANY OF YOUNG CHILDREN IS WHAT KEEPS HER HEART AT PEACE AND HAPPY."

She has learned that this has helped her know her desire for the future; seeing that every child in the streets of SSD has a place to call home. She believes no child desires to be in the road, but due to unavoidable circumstances in life, some find themselves there. Miss Khang says that every child has a right to healthy living plus education, and that a street child does not get access to either.

"It should never be too late for any child. The clock's hand could still be turned to its right hour through desire, hard work, determination, and patience, which is the mother of all."

MEET DENG DUNGA

Model, Actor, Activist, Student!

Dunga was the South Sudanese's face to the world as he represented South Sudan in Mister World 2019 competition, on August 23, 2019, in Manilla, Philippines.

A high fashion model, Deng Dunga also does fashion design. He tries to use his growing recognition to support humanitarian activities that will foster peace, stability, and socio-economic empowerment for the South Sudanese community around the world.

His brands are Dunga Apparel, Sunga Apparel White Party, and Dunga Fashion Show. His appearances on the runway have included such events as Nairobi Fashion Week, Fashion High Tea, Casino Melindi Fashion, Fashion Against Cancer, Luo Festival, and Nairobi Fashion Market.

On the internet, Dunka hosts "The Raw Show," which covers arts, sports, music, fashion and culture. You can find The Raw Show at **http://bit.ly/2QSDdYz**

Deng Dunga is not only a sexy fashion model, but he is also determined to make this a better world.

South Sudan: A Unified Nation or a Conflict of Tribes?

By Adut Makur Athorbei

Arabs to the north and Ethiopia to the southwest, the White Nile flowing through her, and her land rich with the gifts of nature, South Sudan is a unique land. But, is it a land at all? So many tribes, so many languages and dialects, so many regions: can we be one nation?

During the second Anya (1983-2005), ours was still primarily a nation of tribes. Indeed, for many people there was little awareness of even their larger tribal membership. It was enough for most to think in terms of their own village and the villages near them.

The battle to free our nation from Khartoum changed things. Suddenly, large numbers of people were on the move. Fleeing from the aggression of the Arabs or simply identifying with the aspirations of the SPLM, thousands of South Sudanese from different tribes and districts left their homes. Many ended up in refugee camps, at first in Ethiopia and subsequently in Kenya.

While tribal and regional identities didn't disappear in those camps, people were suddenly thrown into contact with other groups. Indeed, camaraderie, a sense of mutual purpose, and an identification with the SPLM brought forth a new sense that we belonged to a single country.

Diversity was to be respected, but unity was clearly more important. Now, many of our people have found their ways around the globe. There are South Sudanese communities in Europe, in Canada and the United States, and in Australia. It makes more sense for the people in those communities to work together to push the cause of our nation forward rather than to continue tribal and regional rivalries from the days before independence.

In our homeland, and especially in the capital city of Juba, it is far more important that we as a people be making common cause than competing one group against another.

Not only has tribalism fueled the horrors that people back home have experienced since independence but it has interfered with forming a cohesive, unifying spirit among those living in diaspora. Ours is a new country and one with many needs. We should be working together rather than fighting one another. Every village, town, and city—no matter where it is located, no matter how far it may be from Juba, no matter what its demographics and tribal composition—must be treated with respect, and every citizen of our country and every one of her children at home or abroad must know that they are valued and will have the assistance of all our people. Whatever our tribe, state, or region, let us remember that the people of South Sudan are one.

Adut Makur Athorbei is a South Sudanese- Canadian Activist based in Ottawa Ontario, Canada. She can be reach at **a.athorbei2011@hotmail.com**

Poems

By Marial Awendit

Abirmuoth

Scars are maps to old songs,
Brewed when tears have no tongues
                To tell of joys.

We shall not word so loud a rock, Abirmuoth.
We are birthed by a land
Where men barter livers
                For drops of honey.

Sometimes we grope
For our fathers in lakes
Of solemn nights and unfiltered echoes
Of bruised laughter.

Echoes of a land where lightning cannot find
 Roots through darkness of crowned hearts.

Sometimes when our fathers bid us farewell
We begin to be sure the moon will find them.
                    We begin to think

The body like the night
Wears its scars as stars.

Like You Woman

Like you, woman,
Writhing on a childbed
Like million needles bit you,
My body is scattered by sharks
Of ravenous longing.

Like you, woman, sometimes
Feeling ground and burnt by fires
Your bone sires,

I am tethered by things
That fill me with honeyed light.

My pledge will not let this string
Of honey slide off my tongue
As the bluebell grows from blue to ashes.

Unlike you, woman,
Turning in the mirror glow for glow,

I clean my hair
Whenever I intend my brain.

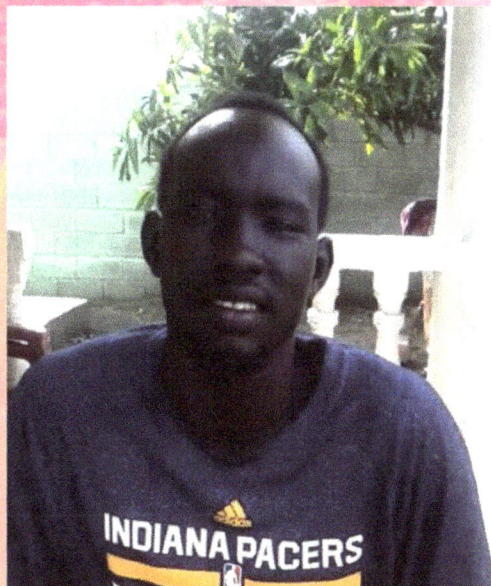

Marial Awendit

is a South Sudanese poet and essayist, born Dec. 1991. He writes from Yirol, Eastern Lakes State. His poems have been published in Brittle Paper, Kalahari Review, AfricanWriter, Praxis Magazine Online, Best New African Poets 2016 Anthology and elsewhere lit. He won the 2018 Babishai-Niwe Poetry Award.

Bongo

By Deng Mayik Atem, Publisher

IF I AM NOT BONGO.
I AM NO ONE!

Tribal identities are a challenge to many societies because the politics of identity drive people apart. South Sudan has sixty plus ethnic groups. From that diversity we must find unity. Our motto should be, "One nation for many." In our homeland, character should count more than region, background, and tribe. One should not have to be from a particular tribe or region to be accepted. What ought to count is an individual's ability to contribute to our society and the decency they bring to their dealings with others.

We must embrace one another for who we are and recognize that pluralism is what can move South Sudan forward. When I joined the Sudan People's Liberation Army and Movement in 1986, I had little understanding of the diversity of our land. I knew of my own tribe, Dinka, and I knew that there were Nuer and Arabs living near my village.

Beyond that I knew nothing of other regions and groups. Now, I know more of the variety and richness of our country, and I celebrate that variety. I hope that you do as well. Of course, our country has gone through some difficult and troubling times. It is easy to understand how frustration, impatience, and ignorance can fuel hatred and allow those who wish to do so to lead us towards negativity and conflict.

Sadly, it is easy for hate and bigotry to take strong root in among us. But, I believe there is still room to create togetherness, to fashion a fabric of mutual respect that will keep our society wrapped in tolerance and pluralism. In order to weave that fabric, we must remember that the smallest of groups deserve the same respect as the largest. In our nation, there are smallest tribes and among them tribes, is the Bongo of the Tonj state in Bahr el Ghazal region. With only about 16, 000 members left in their tribe, the Bongo are few in number, but equally valuable as part of our nation's cultural wealth as any other tribe. That is why I choose to identify with the Bongo people and proclaim that, "If I am not Bongo, I am no one!" By saying this I affirm that if I do not acknowledge the least of my fellows, then I reject my identity as a citizen of South Sudan. Are we not all members of that one tribe?

BONGO A MONUMENTAL
STATUE FROM
SOUTH SUDAN

ELIZABETH CONVENIENT STORE AND HAIR BRAIDING

SO MUCH MORE!

4935 W Glendale Ave, Glendale, AZ 85301
(623) 486-2974

Clothes, Food, Beauty Items, Something for your home! Hair Braiding and more...Come by and see us.

THE ROLE OF SOUTH SUDANESE DIASPORA IN A NATION-BUILDING

By Chol Ajak Demach

First and foremost, I would like to thank Mr. Deng Atem for asking me to write something to our community in Diaspora, and it has taken me while thinking about what is best for me to write about and try to contribute positively to our community, and finally I thought the best thing I can do to help is to try to highlight the role of Diaspora in nation-building and I don't claim in anyway to be an expert on the subject matter but is my humble tried to drew from my own experience as

someone who was once part of the diaspora community and now working and living back home in South Sudan, and sees how this experience and other Communities experiences can help guide our community to play a better roles in nation-building. Without a doubt the South Sudanese diaspora community in United States of America, has played a big role in contributing to Independence of South Sudan, through lobbying the host country Government and highlighting the suffering of the

people of Southern Sudan, wish let to the passing of the Sudan peace Act (Pub.l107-245) and signed into law on On Sept 21, 2002 the President of the United States of America, George W Bush, signed the Sudan Peace Act into law. That law led the way to the signing of the Comprehensive Peace Agreement in 2005 and subsequently to the independence of our country on July 9, 2011. Mr. Bush's signature on that law represented the culmination of great effort on the part of South Sudanese in the United States

DIASPORA'S RESPONSIBILITY TO SOUTH SUDAN

an effort that had included lobbying for the law and making sure that the people and the government of the United States understood the suffering of our people under Sudanese control.

After independence, many members of the diaspora in the U.S. and in other countries felt that the job was done, that independence had put Juba in the right direction. Sadly, there was and continues to be much more to be done. Although I have returned to our homeland, I am still in contact with people in the States and throughout the diaspora and I want to use the kind invitation of Ramciel Magazine to share my views to deliver a call to my compatriots around the world. There is still much nation building to be done. The diaspora community has much to do.

First, there is the economic contribution. Many South Sudanese living in other countries send money back to our nation. Much of it is help for family members and others who need assistance. That money makes a great difference, especially in smaller communities where there is so little. And, when it goes to assist young people to get an education, it is not just an economic boost but a contribution to our country's future.

Many South Sudanese living in other countries dream of returning to our mother land. Some are already having houses built, which is another great contribution to our nation's economy. Some are trying to establish businesses that will connect the South Sudanese economy to other countries.

Sadly, others are not thinking about the near future; they talk of returning to Africa but actually allow themselves to be caught in the 40/40 trap: work forty hours a week for forty years and then they will die poor and still trapped in America or whatever country in which they live.

Often those people who are working so diligently are active members of their local South Sudanese communities. They take part in the festivals and contribute to the fund-raisers. Sadly, they have not thought ahead and have not planned how to get the most good from the money they contribute. They have not considered investing in small businesses back in South Sudan.

They are not contributing to local infrastructure efforts such as building schools, health clinics, and fisheries. They are no looking for ways to help the agriculture back in their home villages, for example by digging better wells or helping their families to see beyond cattle raising as a form of development. One of the things that local communities in other nations can do that would be particularly helpful would be creating community associations that have legal standing as companies back home in South Sudan. Then those associations could become active agents in local economic development.

When community associations in the diaspora become economic agents back home, they can hire staff, which means helping those who have studied to use their educations for good. It also means that there is leverage to push local communities towards change.

as the shareholders and hire some people with experience to runs these companies , and by doing so we can realize the great benefits that will come out of this projects interim of jobs curation for the local and help in changing the future of our nation, we can't leave everything for the government to do or wait till things get better before we think of doing our part, and in many actions it has been proven that the government is not a solution but rather the government is the problem, therefore we must go around it and develop our nation with the resources we have, and also by doing the above mention project you will be   securing your future and the future of our children's, financially, second to that the first generation can start to come home and utilize the experiences gain in states in helping our people, am not here talking about government jobs but rather talking of doing the work for private business in the field of your choices, and by the way many like me have taken that decision and made the joinery home and start using the experiences learned, in all areas like media, and health sector and NGO's and business entrepreneurs, and aviation fields etc.

As a results I can say without a doubt that our contribution as a returnee from Diaspora has made our country little better than we found it, and I will like to encourage the government of South Sudan to engage the Diaspora and find the ways, to utilize the human resources and financial contribution of the Diaspora and create a diaspora department that can help channel in all the efforts, and make diasporas contribution in nation-building more effective.

The second group I will call them the second generation South Sudanese American, and those are the one born and went to school in America and know nothing about South Sudan other than the stories they hear from their parents or from the community events, we will be doing them a great service if we start to teach them South Sudan's native languages and the history and plan for them to visit home once in awhile and this will impact them greatly, and in turn they will be of greater help to our nation in the future, and the evidence is there, just look to the State of Israel today and how powerful it is, and it's all because of the Jews American and their present in all level of American government and business and their tight connection to Israel , so let help our kids to achieve their American dreams while knowing about their heritage, and where they came from because it help Sharpe them for future and President Obama example is not far away and how is connection to Africa and his first visit to his father home in Kenya help him and make him feel proud about his family history, please read his book "The Dream from my father" adding to that we can see country like Ghana has open the doors for the African American who want o t return to African and give them home, since they don't know from which part of Africa they were taken during the slavery time, and we can avoid that dilemma for our kids since we all know our history and passed it down to them, and it will not be a bad idea for Diaspora to create a data base web for South Sudanese that will have all the families information's from the family tree and the day of arrival to States, etc.

By doing so, we will be helping the next generations of South Sudanese and keep them connected to the motherland. Finally, some of the great benefits of returning home that I enjoy very much with the other from Diaspora that returned home is eating all fresh and organic foods and drinking milk and eating the honey; we are really the land of milk and honey as stated in the bible. Let's all work in Diaspora and back home for the betterment of our nation and play our small roles and may God bless South Sudan.

Finally, as those new economic entities come into their own, the members from around the world will have an opportunity to return to their homeland and to take part in that activity. This means that the skills our people have learned in other countries will now have a role in South Sudan.

As the people of the diaspora become more economically and socially active, that will in turn bring pressure on the governments in Juba and the various states to work towards change and growth. The voices of our people will be magnified by our actions.

Of course, many of the diaspora don't know our motherland. Their parents having left during the war years, they were born in other countries. They are the second generation South Sudanese Americans, Canadians, Australians, etc.

What do they know of South Sudan? We have a responsibility to teach them their/our heritage. We have a responsibility to not only tell them our stories and teach them our languages and songs but also to encourage them to return to their homeland and to be connected to our nation. It is important to know who one is and from where they came as part of knowing the dignity of life.

Chol Ayuen is Former Secretary-General of the SPLM Chapter of Arizona from 2006-2007, a member of the First SPLM diaspora conference in Juba 2007, and Currently a managing Director of Zas Juba Ltd. Mr. Ayuen holds a Bachelor of Law from Cairo University Khartoum Branch.

Akoul Ngong Malek

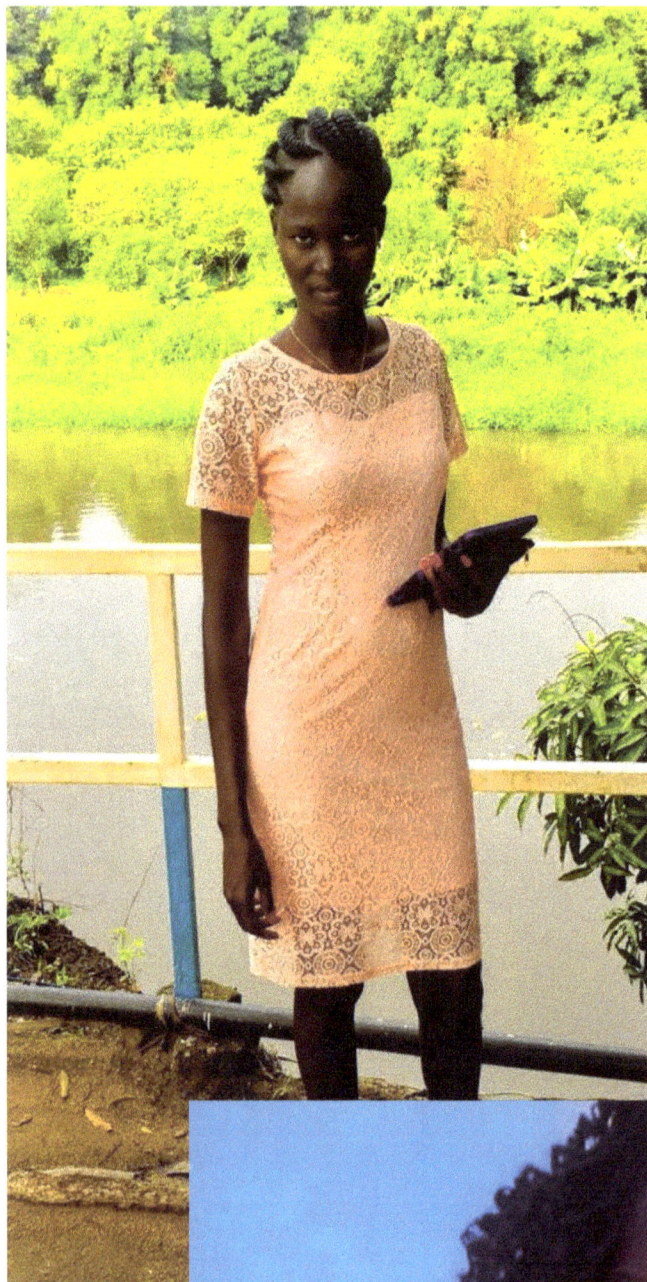

Akuol Ngong Malek, Alumnus of Methodist University of Kenya, model, activist, and founder of South Sudan Talent show (SSTS).

Miss Malek first thought about SSTS in childhood. She has always wanted to highlight and promote the talents and aspirations of the youth of South Sudan. SSTS promotes many skills including sports, music, modeling, comedy, and beauty pageantry.

The core objective of SSTS is to highlight and promote the South Sudanese Youths with talents and aspirations. The skills that SSTS promotes included but not limited to sports, music, modeling, comedy, beauty pageant, and many more.

This year's award show in Juba saw a host of exceptional and accomplished young people perform. You can follow SSTS on Facebook. http://bit.ly/2FGhMDD

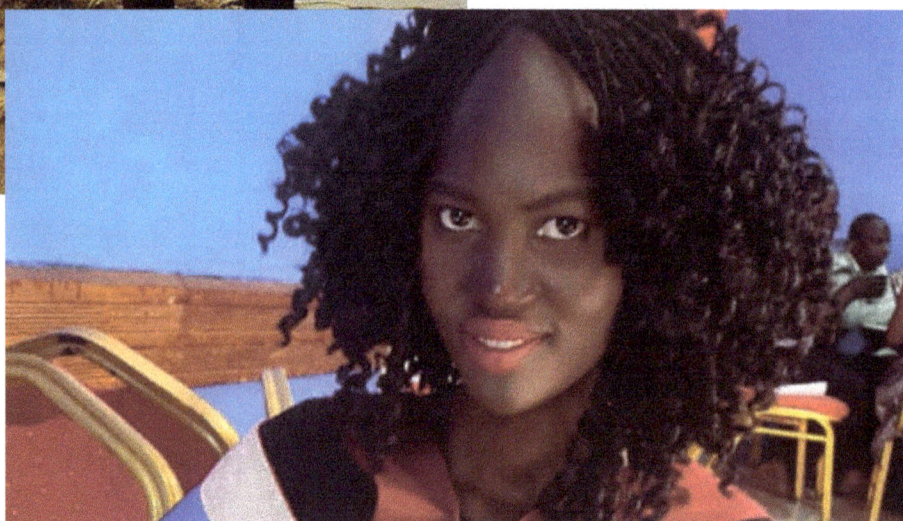

ASARA BULLEN'S INTERVIEW WITH THE HONORABLE LAM TUNGWAR KUEIWONG

Northern Liech State's Minister of Youths and Sports and a former minister in the same position in Unity State which is now defunct. Former president of the National Youths of South Sudan as well former chairperson of South Sudan's Artists Association and a founder of Miss Malikia of South Sudan and Talent Success of South Sudan.

Asara: Who is Lam Tungwar? Hon. Lam Tungwar: In simple terms - Lam is my home name. I don't have a well-known Christian name such as Peter. Lam was the name given to me by my parents. I'm from Bentiu.

Asara: You were a musician? Hon. Lam Tungwar: I am a musician - music is part of me. It is a skill, a talent, and it is something that I'm passionate about. I'm famous among our people because of my expertise in music, and I used that as a platform for doing activist work. I did a lot of performances as well. Also, I had the opportunity to visit foreign countries where I met many faces and inspiring individuals with whom I shared the history of our struggle I was among those who were tasked with the purpose of highlighting and informing the world about why South Sudan should be the country of South Sudan,

and Sudan should be the separate country of Sudan. That is a good reason why we should be divided. We were the voices of the people of South Sudan representing them through music; talking and meeting people who did not know us. We disseminated our cause.

Asara: What was it like to be a minister during the conflict? Hon. Lam Tungwar: That was tough because the conflict had broken a lot of the social fabric, you know, from family to family. Like right now, for example, my elder brother and I, we are in different camps.

Our politics do not match, and it is because of the conflict. It was in a time when tribal tendency had reached different heights as a result of the 2013 conflicts. The tribal trend comes out of everybody's heart, and social media made it worse. When people see you working with the government, people branded me and themselves. We were poisoned by social media. There were a lot of dirty things. Tribal hatred and so many other animosities had re-surfaced.

It is not suitable for our generation, especially our youth. I was appointed in a time when there was an ongoing fight between the government of South Sudan and the rebels. All the warring parties were fighting to overtake the government. I didn't support those who stood up against the system that was set-up by all of us. I'm one of those who didn't like fighting, but I was battling most of those who defected and took sides with the rebels, although I did share ethnicity in terms of the tribe with them, but not ideology.

There have been so many personal attacks on me, especially on social media. People talk about things that are not okay, and they try to discourage you and your cause, and what you are doing. I believe among the sixty-four tribes there is no lesser tribe among them. All of them are better and equal. The Republic of South Sudan's constitution was set by all of us and a president that was elected by all of us. So it wasn't a time for us to engage in another conflict. After all, we had just liberated ourselves from Sudan after decades of civil wars. We should be telling our people that "because of your wishes" and the idea that your tribe will back you up, shouldn't be the pretext of starting a conflict. It doesn't make sense at all.

So this conflict and being appointed at the time of the war had brought a lot of devastation to me at a personal level as well as to my work. It is hard to make people understand when they grow up with a lot of hate in them. So it is a severe cause, to make some of them understand what others think about. It is about individuals who polarize for their interests, their gain, and confuse others by saying that the conflict was a tribal war, which it is not a tribal war. It is just a function of disagreement.

Asara: Who was the most difficult person you've dealt with? How did you manage the situation? Hon. Lam Tungwar: I was in the middle. I dealt with relevant issues, multiple relevant issues.

Not one person, but chiefs, government, military, and militias. There are multi-groups whom I dealt with, but you see how tough it is to convince somebody full of hate, who is tribal in his own heart.

His own heart, or character, believes others shouldn't exist. That was the "most challenging part," but we have to make sure that we make them understand that the cause is there. It is not a common thing. Is not about you, me, or not about hating and killing children, burning houses; these are not things we want to encourage in South Sudan. South Sudan has come a long way. We have had twenty-one years of war.

Asara: Can you name someone who had a significant impact on you as a leader? Hon. Lam Tungwar: Yes. I have multiple people who have had an impact on me, and they have that impact because of the substance they carry with them and that has changed my life. One of those people is my father.

My father is a very excellent man. He has been chief since 1936 and up to now. He is an 87-year-old paramount chief and still going strong.

He knows the government from day one, since the independence of Sudan, colonial time, and until the liberation by the SPLA/M of 1983. He is aware of everything. He knows very well what government looks like and what it does. My father is my inspiration.

Another person is Dr. John Garang, the founder of the SPLA/M. He had some different ideas, but he understood the movement, understood the South Sudanese. John understood every tribe in South Sudan. He had learned from each of us as an educated man, which is one of the things that inspired me the most about Dr. John Garang. When he was in Kapoeta with lower the villagers, Garang would lower himself.

He would be like them. If he went to another area, he would go into the rural areas and meet the average person, discuss things at their level and not at his level. He was a person who understood a lot about our people. A good example was when he appointed governors, he made sure that if you were from

Nuer he would send you to Kapoeta. If you were a Dinka you might be sent somewhere else. If it had been John Garang continuing to lead us the system of governors could have been different.

He believed anyone could help manage somewhere. You don't have to be from Jonglei to manage Jonglei or from Kuacjok, Wau, or elsewhere. He was the guy who had a lot for the unity of South Sudan.

Asara: Tell us about your music career? I believe you and Emmanuel Jal were in one band sometime back in Kenya? Hon: Lam Tungwar: Yes, He was my guy. We were in a group.

Asara: How did you link up with Emmanuel Jal? Hon. Lam Tungwar: Emmanuel, me, and another guy called Matthew were in a band together. The three of us started out in Kenya. We were branded lost boys of Sudan. We were the Red Army and the Red Army was scattered over many areas.

Some of us were in Pinyudio, Itang, and Duma, Plataka, Narus, and, later on, Kakuma Refugee Camp in Kenya, but we were the people of Pinyudo and others were from Duma. Most of the Red Army were brought to Kukama. So Jal and I met first in Kukama, and later on, we met in school in Nairobi. He and I are relatives.

His father and my father are from Nhiladau in the former Unity State in the Upper Nile region. Our fathers had been close friends for a long time, even during the liberation struggle, and they knew each other.

So when we came together we had the same ideas for writing, like writing poem. Jal, of course, is the guy who loves to sing. Me, I like writing drama, staging things, acting and all that. We found out that we had some things in common that we could do. We talked about the history of the lost boys, the Red Army, and we went ahead and wrote about it. I think that was where the ideas came from.

Someone like Matthew was with us as a part of the band and he wasn't a child-soldier like us. But he came to love the story of the child-soldier and the lost boys. He sees himself in the category of a young man who, from thin and sticks, survived in the Jungle and arrived safely. With that our music is conscious, although it has changed over time.

I don't know how Jal is doing now. But the music then was about peace, unity, and about South Sudanese who should have the right to live and shouldn't be chased out of their territories, shouldn't be killed. The South Sudanese need opportunities for everything - health, education, and right to live their lives.

Our music was very much about social issues, the practical social issues we face. We were the people who were boosting the morale behind the Sudan People Liberation Army/Movement, who were fighting on the frontline. The SPLA was fighting for the right causes, good ideas, and safety of our people. Jal and I were very much there in that environment.

Asara: Tell me about how you met LL Cool J.
Hon. Lam Tungwar: Well, I met LL Cool J, TI, Steven Spielberg, and several other inspiring folks through the U.S. State Department. Especially LLCool J, I met him in Los Angeles. We talked about the need to support Africa, and South Sudan in particular. He said to me, "Lam, I have this massive heart for humanity, and the only

problem is - how do I get to help you guys and how do I reach you? What can I do?"

To my surprise, this is the guy who had learned about us even before we met him. I think his public relations team had explained much about us to him. So I asked him if he could come to South Sudan? He told me, "Lam, I wouldn't be able to go to South Sudan.

I can only come to South Africa or Europe, which are the places where you can get more crowds to attend the concerts. You can raise enough money for the suffering children in South Sudan." That was the first thing we touched upon. We talked a lot about humanity, and he talked a lot about how he needs to help humankind in whatever capacity he can. He dedicated two percent of his music career to people around the world who are vulnerable.

This connection with him was through the U.S. State Department, and that was how I met Mr. LLCool J. It was a pleasure to meet him, and up to today we are still in contact, but due to conflict everything fell apart. Otherwise, whatever we discussed could have had yielded tangible results.

Currently, LL Cool J and I are still communicating. He sometimes checks on me, asks about the situation and how things are coming along because he keeps hearing about the continuation of the conflict in the country.

Asara: How did you meet Mandela in Washington?
Hon. Lam Tungwar: Yes, through Young African Leadership. I was there for two events which were in Washington, D.C. I went for young African leaders, and I did civic education and leadership through various universities in the USA. My education was about how US politics evolved. Two hundred plus years, and the US had come a long way, and how there are still challenges right now as compared to South Sudan, which is just four years old from its independence.

Which country in this world has two armies? Who are those guys with arms? Who are these guys with guns? It is difficult, but this revitalized accord is a completely united factor where Dr. Riek Machar will come and serve under the leadership of TGNU just like anyone, and that will be the same for the military generals. Those generals will serve in the Army under the guidance of President Salva Kiir Mayardit.

Everybody in their quarter will have to follow one order in one system. This revitalizes, and also stimulates, a lot. Now it is time for the South Sudanese to be done with rebellion, especially running out and coming back. That one is not making sense. So far, they are tired, and it should be the time to do politics instead of war.

Salva Kiir Mayardit spearheaded this revitalized peace, and he is working hard to make sure it works out well. He is monitoring it day and night, and I believe it will work because our people are tired of war, and they know very well there should be no reason to continue to fight each other. Innocent people suffered tremendously and there is no reason to subject people to such heinous pain in the first place.

Advertise Your Business With Ramciel Magazine

SPOTLIGHT ON A YOUNG JOURNALIST

Marko Makat Deng remembers watching his father's cattle as a boy in the village of Wungop. He also remembers his father listening to the news on a transistor radio. The voices that came out of that little box fascinated Marko and the fact that his father listened so intently to them made them seem even more important than the voices of the people whom he heard talking every day. So fascinated was the little boy that he made himself a toy radio and pretended that he too was listening to the news.

It was only when he went to school that that Marko learned the word for those people talking on the radio, journalist. From that day, he wanted to make journalism his career. That career choice was reinforced when young Marko watched SSTV, which is now SSBC-TV. He loved to watch Garang John and knew that he wanted to do the news with the same skill and gravitas.

In 2016, Marko had the opportunity to study journalism and radio presentation at the Yei Educational Professional Skills Centre, where he completed a three-month certificate. Now, he is continuing his studies in journalism and mass communication at the University of Juba.

Having discovered the internet and Facebook, Marko began posting stories in 2016. In 2017, he created Twic Media Reports as his platform for reaching a larger audience. His goal from the start has been to offer grassroots journalism, stories from local communities that should be heard by the rest of South Sudan and the world.

Usually, such stories are ignored by the national and international press. While Marko is from Twic State, TMR is not limited to Twic alone. He tries to cover the surrounding states as well.

Sometimes, but not regularly, he also tries to report on national news. But, always, the emphasis is on stories from smaller communities and of course how outside events will affect those communities.
Of course, politics is part of TMR's coverage, but Marko wants to cover humanity.

He wants to encourage peace, education, economic growth, and of course sports and culture. His view is that journalism must not just address problems but also share and support what is positive. That said, he does want to use his voice to fight corruption, to support human rights, to encourage equal education for women, and especially to fight gender-based violence.

Although Marko sees the future of journalism being primarily on the internet, he still loves radio broadcasting and hopes to expand TMR both online and on-air. So far, Marko has carried the full weight of supporting TMR on his own shoulders, but he hopes that others will see its importance and contribute.

Not only does he need equipment, but he also needs ways to encourage him many volunteer reporters from local communities. It is they who provide the trustworthy, accurate and impartial information that Marko prizes.

Marko Makat Deng can be found on Facebook or by messaging him at Ramciel Magazine. For a young man of only twenty-six he has already proven himself as a South Sudanese who has much to offer

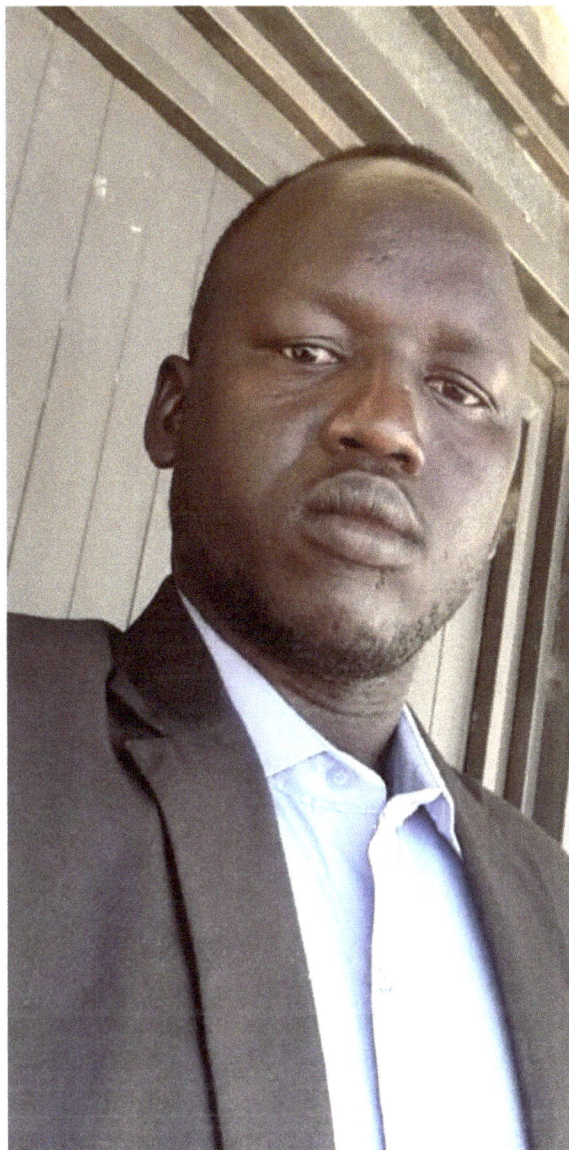

DEPORTATION: HUNDREDS OF SOUTH SUDANESE FORCED FROM THE UNITED STATES

By Deng Mayik Atem

More than 50,000 people have left South Sudan and moved to the United States. Most of them came by way of the refugee camps.

Perhaps there would be less sense of us as a group and we would be more assimilated into the American population, especially the Black American world, if it were not for the "Lost Boys and Lost girls" who were allowed to come to the US in early 2000.

That group of approximately 3,800 young people were allowed to come to the States in 2001. They served as a catalyst to remind us
all of our African heritage.

Of course, most of the people who came to the United States did so before 2011, which means that when they arrived they were identified as citizens of Sudan. At the time, that was not a problem.

Now, however, there has been a change. The Trump administration has labeled Sudan as part of the swamp that must be drained. Mr. Trump identified eight countries from which nationals were banned from entering the United States.

Sudan was one of them. Of course, it is ironic that our country with its great sudd was not labeled as part of the swamp. Our citizens are still allowed to enter the U.S.A. In large part, that is because most of us are Christians not Muslims and few of us identify as Arabs.

Be that as it may, we South Sudanese living in America still have a problem. Many of us have become American citizen, but many have not.

Often, they have avoided applying for citizenship because they were intimidated by the test.

Some were not allowed citizenship or had their applications delayed because of minor criminal infractions, insufficient to have them deported but serious enough to delay citizenship.

Most of them have never applied to have their green cards changed; they are still listed as Sudanese. Of course, as soon as they run afoul of the law, that label opens them for quick deportation. While some may be repeat offenders or have committed serious crimes, many of the people who are deported would have been allowed to stay had their papers said they came from South Sudan.

This is particularly true of those who have been arrested for drug possession. The saddest thing is that many of these deportees are young men—yes far more men than women—who have spent far more of their lives in America than in South Sudan.

While they may not be fluent English speakers and may not have done as well in school as might be hoped, they are certainly more American than African. Yet, off they are shipped to a country in which they are unprepared to live and which is unprepared to take them in. What a sad commentary on our times.

Recently, I visited Juba. A few days before I left to return to my home in America, I learned that a group of young South Sudanese deportees had arrived in Juba. Four of them were from my home state of Arizona. In that state, I work for the legal system as an interpreter. I deal with many such cases.

Based on that experience, I encourage South Sudanese living in the States to apply for citizenship and to make sure that their green cards indicate that they are from South Sudan. Once the system has an individual in its sights, it is too late to get the situation corrected.

The Plight of the South Sudan Woman

By Nyabuoy Gatbel

On March 8, 2019, on Women's Day, I thought about the plight of South Sudanese women; our history and our contemporary struggle. We often have our indigenous Nilotic and Bantu issues labeled through the lens of 'the western gaze' and the rhetoric that has been pushed out. The South Sudanese women's plight has to be seen in a proper historical context, not relying solely on contemporary western information.

Today's South Sudanese women's issues are rooted in multiple colonizations stemming from the dynastic period during the reign of ancient Egypt, Nubia and Kush. During those multiple colonizations of the Ottoman Turks, Arabs, Greek, Roman and European the image of the Nilotic and Bantu women became redefined. She went from ruling beside her men to being demoted in the eyes of the colonizers.

 These colonizers brought their own definitions of beauty, womanhood, and proper gender conduct. The gender values and constructs deeply rooted in their own societies were then imposed upon the African woman. The African people became a conquered people and, as a result, the image of the African woman became defined and controlled by the colonizers

Photo Credit - Vanessa Parra/Oxfam

> "We often have our indigenous Nilotic and Bantu issues labeled through the lens of 'the western gaze' and the rhetoric that has been pushed out."

Today's South Sudanese women's issues are rooted in multiple colonizations stemming from the dynastic period during the reign of ancient Egypt, Nubia and Kush. During those multiple colonizations of the Ottoman Turks, Arabs, Greek, Roman and European the image of the Nilotic and Bantu women became redefined. She went from ruling beside her men to being demoted in the eyes of the colonizers.

These colonizers brought their own definitions of beauty, womanhood, and proper gender conduct. The gender values and constructs deeply rooted in their own societies were then imposed upon the African woman. The African people became a conquered people and, as a result, the image of the African woman became defined and controlled by the colonizers.

The image colonizers had of African women has lead to an inferiorization of African women in cultural space, politics, religion, and overall African society. As the image and characteristics of foreign women became the dominant force in African society, the reduction of African women lead to a downfall of the collective society. Conquer the image of women to control the narrative of the country.

The narrative from the colonial perspective has cheapened the role of African women internationally and globally. We must understand the strategic mechanisms applied to understand how the African woman's image continues to be colonized till this day. For the authentic image of the African Nilotic and Bantu women to emerge, the image has to be decolonized, healed, and promoted in an empowering way. Authentic change comes from unearthing the true history of our women in antiquity to understand the contemporary plight.

Please find Nyabuoy Gatbel's website below and use her bio for the Article The Plight of South Sudanese Women. **http://bit.ly/2Rhyr5Z**

Write for Ramciel Magazine
INFO@RAMCIELMAGAZINE.COM

"South Sudanese women's issues are rooted in multiple colonizations stemming from the dynastic period during the reign of ancient Egypt, Nubia and Kush...

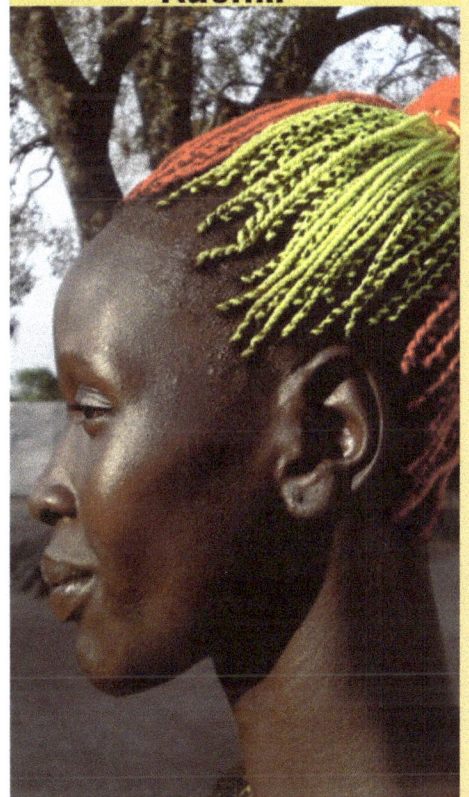

In Honor of My Mother and All the Mothers of South Sudan A View from Australia

By Adol Makeny Dhieu

From all corners of our beautiful South Sudan, we come, we Nilotic women. Perhaps we draw our strength from Mother Nile. Perhaps it is from the soil of our native Africa. We march with pride and resilience. We strive for the greater causes of freedom and equality while carrying our children in search of shelter and safe haven. We, the women of South Sudan, epitomize the strength of the black woman.

During the years of war, while men were often absent, our mothers raised us, the millennials who are now raising our own children. Not only did our mothers raise us, but they instilled in us the audacity of hope, the freedom of spirit, and the capacity to dream big. They taught us the values of hard work and dedication.

With hope, our mothers endured the worst days of the civil war. With hope, they struggled to get us safely to refugee camps. Typically, they made that arduous journey without their husbands. It was their capacity for hope and their belief in the power of humanity to come to the aid of those in need that sustained them during the worst of times.

"In adversity our mothers discovered their strength and their resiliency."

Even when they had brought us to the safety of humanitarian camps in other countries, they did not stop their efforts to teach us a sense of energy and urgency, a determination to make our lives and the future of our nation count. They pushed us to obtain educations and to learn what the modern world had to offer. When I arrived in Australia sixteen years ago, one of my goals was to graduate from university, a goal I proudly achieved. At the same time, our mothers reminded us of our traditions and of the dignity of our past.

Sadly, for some of us, their mothers were left behind. It was a testimony to our mothers' generation that those who were lonely so often found support and love from other women whom they met along the way. Our traditional values of caring for others, of welcoming and sharing with strangers were never forgotten. Now, we millennial women, many of us flung around the world in a great diaspora, have become mothers. We face the tasks of adapting to life in the twenty-first century and doing so in new lands while raising our children to remember and honor our homeland and our culture left behind.

As my mother raised me, I now raise my four children. In my efforts to bring them up as proud South Sudanese, I speak our tribal language at home, I prepare traditional food such as combo and Asida. I play records of our music and encourage them to sing and dance along. It is important that they should grow up proud of our heritage. I know that we the women of South Sudan are up to the challenge. We were raised to be strong, strong like our mothers. We-are an embodiment of the heritage of strong South Sudanese women who have cared for their children and their children's children since time began.

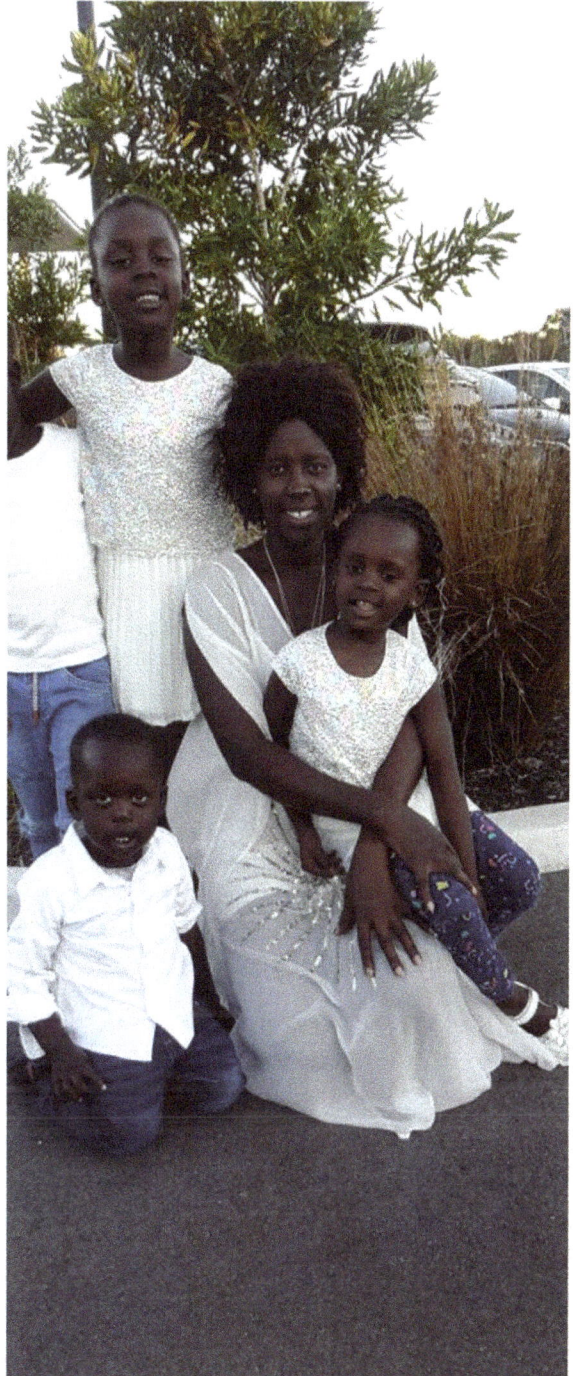

Adol Makeny Dhieu is a South Sudanese - Australian Lawyer. She was recently admitted to the Supreme Court of New South Wales as a lawyer. She can be reach at **adolamckeny@gmail.com**

Sending Our Dead

HOME TO SOUTH SUDAN?

By Deng Mayik Atem

Long ago, when Plague was ravishing Europe, people with carts would roam through the cities and towns, calling, "Bring out your dead." They would be wearing masks that looked like birds of prey in the belief that those masks would keep them safe from the poisonous vapors being given off by the dead. We share this bit of history because we want our readers to know we realize that dealing with death is one of the most difficult things we humans do. Every group, every religion, every tribe has developed their own ways of dealing with the dead.

It is one of the things that marks us the human species, and that we so universally wrestle with death. Respecting and dignifying the deceased is what makes us human beings. It is right that we honor deceased family, friends, relatives, and even strangers.

 The specifics of how we honor the deceased varies from community to community. Some are mourned for days, weeks, or even months. When some die, their deaths are a time for animal sacrifice and great feasts. For some, death is marked by prayer. Again, that is as it should be.

Again, that is as it should be. There is no one right way to say goodbye, no one correct way to mourn. Many people, not just from South Sudan but all over the world, prefer that the remains of the dead be buried with their own families in their home villages. Of course, when the deceased have left their home community and settled many miles away, perhaps even on the other side of the world, returning their remains for burial becomes a major task, one that is costly and stressful. Dying can be a very expensive process, especially in the United States, Australia, Europe, or other places far from South Sudan. There are usually hospital and medical bills, funeral home expenses for preparation of the body and for a casket, and then, if the remains are to be sent back to South Sudan, the great expense of shipping that body home.

If friends and family want to have the deceased sent home, another problem is that with the best of luck it will take two weeks. Just keeping the body ready for transportation adds more expense. Worse, it is often a conflict between the wish to provide optimum dignity for the departed and placing them into what amounts as storage. Is it worth doing this? Is it worth spending the money? Should South Sudanese who have died in the Diaspora be returned to South Sudan? Of course, that is a decision made by those closest to the deceased. For some families, there is plenty of money, even enough so relatives who live nearby can return to South Sudan with the remains. For some, this is a great burden and they should not be condemned for being unable to pay that high freight.

There is another consideration that deserves discussion. Not all who die would want their remains to be repatriated to South Sudan. Many of the younger members of our Diaspora have spent little of their lives in our homeland, and even less in their families' traditional villages. They may identify more with their homes in the Diaspora than anyplace in South Sudan. Moreover, because so many of our people have moved away from their traditional villages, the deceased may not even be welcomed back. There may not be a distant relative willing to arrange the burial.

Meanwhile, there may be other people living in the Diaspora who are close to the deceased and want their remains close by. It may seem respectful to ship the body back to Juba, and from there on to some village, but it may actually be exactly the opposite of the truly respectful act of burying somebody in their Diaspora home.

Often collections are made among the members of a community to arrange for the shipping of a body back to South Sudan for burial. It may cost as much as $30,000 or more, which is an astounding amount for most people. Perhaps an alternative plan might be to send some of that money back to the family in South Sudan so they can hold an appropriate mourning process, give some to the family in the Diaspora to help with final bills and perhaps lost income, and even using a little of it to help the village from which the deceased's family came to improve its infrastructure. Somehow, digging a hole in the ground to bury someone who died thousands of miles away weeks earlier seems an inferior celebration of their life, rather than digging a well that would allow the village access to fresh water.

Rituals for the deceased may need to change with how times have changed. Finding a way to honor the deceased as well as to honor the family in the Diaspora and in South Sudan can bring the two communities closer together, and provide a healing that is long past due.

THE USIP SPONSOR DIASPORA DIALOGUE

by David Dau Achuoth,Executive Director/Founder of CoSSAR

After gaining independence in 2011 from Sudan, South Sudan relapsed into brutal internal conflict in December 2013. Just six years later, the world's newest nation is now at a critical juncture. Ethnic relations have exponentially worsened, leading to suspicions and mistrust amongst the communities, and the consequences are far-reaching.

The South Sudanese diaspora communities are each other throats due to the conflict. Moreover, they have been affected psychologically by the conflict. Many from the diaspora lost their family members and friends. Such situations used as the pretext for involvement in the conflict.

The role of the diaspora as a financial lifeline for the people of South Sudan is well recognized in South Sudan and globally. However, the diaspora's contribution extends beyond the economic sphere. Their involvement in the conflict ranges from financial contributions and social remittances to lobbying of US policymakers.

South Sudanese diaspora communities around the world have increasingly voiced their grievances through social media, often using inflammatory language and images. The diaspora has fueled the conflict using inflammatory and divisive language on social media and other outlets.

Revitalized Agreement on the Resolution of the Conflict in South Sudan

The information that they choose to share online, via phone, and through social media is a direct line to their family and friends within the country. The polarization amongst the diaspora within the United States is a crucial concern that poses a challenge to bringing sustainable peace and reconciliation to South Sudan.

Although it is imperfect, the Revitalized Agreement on the Resolution of the Conflict in South Sudan (R-ARCSS) was signed in Addis Ababa in September 2018. However, at this stage, the most pressing issue for the South Sudanese in the diaspora is how can they contribute to bringing peace to South Sudan rather than further dividing the country.

The role of the diaspora is critical to both stopping the violence and adding the ongoing peace process, as witnessed during the 2011 referendum in which the diaspora mobilized and overwhelmingly voted for separation.

Therefore, in the interest of peace and reconciliation in the diasporas, a diaspora dialogue aims at promoting inclusivity and durable reconciliation was initiated by the Council on South Sudanese American Relations. The goal was to create a more suitable platform where members of the diaspora would have civil discourse about the 2013 conflict.

Through this project, a core group of ten diaspora leaders received certification training for dialogue facilitation at the United States Institute of Peace. The USIP works with the diaspora facilitators to develop a conceptual framework that is a guide for each dialogue. That shed light on the different factors influencing the diaspora's lack of contributions to peace in South Sudan.

The dialogue aims at enhancing civil discourse with the ultimate goal of advancing social cohesion and social stability through fostering collaborative discussion with participants. These activities are carried out through the lens of four schemes; training on civil communication between people of different tribes, Social media and the impact of hate speech and cyber-bullying. Reconciliation and forgiveness, and Community acceptance.

THE SOUTH SUDANESE DIASPORA DIALOGUE WAS DESIGN USING THE USIP TRAINING MANUAL

In order to deepen the understanding of disunion among the diaspora communities, the South Sudanese diaspora dialogue was design using the USIP training manual but adding a creative metric of implementation. The approach aimed to cover in detail topics related to community reconciliation and forgiveness, as well as to focus on trauma and truth building. The USIP training guide illustrates theoretical and pedagogical questions and methods on community dialogue design using relevant examples from previous community dialogues.

Participants credited the dialogue process for educating them about the impact of hate speech and cyber-bullying on social media. They also acknowledge the importance of civil discussion concepts, which encourage the community and religious leaders to speak to one another about issues facing the diaspora community. The dialogue also shows a positive impact on community leaders by demonstrating that differences or conflicts among community members can be managed and resolved peacefully.

This program also helps participants promote the community's relationship in the sense of being heard and understood while gaining new insight and understanding of the perspectives of others.

DIALOGUE ACTIVITIES: Participants at each of our dialogue were divided into small groups to discuss the processes and principles of dialogue. Each group was asked to take one or two elements and discuss them to come up with detailed responses. During each dialogue, the partakers were not more than 6- 12 participants.

KEY FINDINGS: Conversations revealed essential insights on trauma and community challenges facing the diaspora. In all, we heard from more than 700 participants about how to best promote social cohesion while addressing challenges face by the diaspora community. While the ideas were voluminous, common themes emerged: A base level of anxiety regarding the future of South Sudan The effects of war and its challenges on Diaspora populations repeatedly surfaced. Uncertainties and troublesome decisions in the political realm compound this base level of anxiety felt across the communities.

Across the board, participants from each of the dialogue expressed a desire to form the "South Sudanese Community Association." The associations will be a task with responsibilities to help built community trust and hold and find ways to help South Sudanese learn to participate in their communities. Also, to help South Sudanese Americans assimilate into the secular American society. Moreover, participants and community leaders promise to continue the dialogue in their local communities with supervision and support from the USIP and CoSSAR trained facilitators. CoSSAR and its facilitators will help create the selection guideline for community election focus mainly on tribal diversity, gender diversity, and familiarity with IRS non-profit operational requirements in the U.S.

Increased focus on building community trust Where people live is at the core of their daily lives. Formations of community association will provide safe community environments where members could enjoy common refrain. Participants focus on the discussions about the concentration of building people to people reconciliation approach to conflict prevention, mitigation, management, and peace building in South Sudan. The idea is to help to reinforced awareness of compounded conflict disparities across tribal, ethnic, and socioeconomic lines amongst the diaspora's communities.

SUBMISSIONS   Write for Ramciel Magazine
INFO@RAMCIELMAGAZINE.COM

Need for shared information the Roundtable forums highlighted the never-ending need for frequent communications. At points throughout the dialogues, participants revealed they were not aware of how negative their social media activities were affecting fellow South Sudanese in other communities.

While some spoke explicitly about the need for continuing dialogue between communities' leaders, others talked about how such an initiative could better tell the story of trauma as a health issue. Social media is critically understood as prized and necessary for increased collaboration.

Main Themes: While common themes emerged throughout our listening, there were also clear takeaways from each dialogue that comprises places where dialogue took place. Each had unique issues and ideas on how to collaborate and address concerns about bringing sustainable peace to South Sudan. A full list of "big ideas," developed by participants at each forum, is listed in its entirety will be published when this initiative has ended.

What We Heard: The following feedback and recommendations, specific to facilitators, were derived from a dinner meeting with community leaders and community dialogue forums.

Sharing of community dialogue feedback Participants asked how facilitators would share and use the information generated by this dialogue process and requested the results to be summarized and shared with the public.

In addition to creating this report, participants requested updates with the key findings. Feedback gleaned during community forums will also be a key component of determining our 2019- 2020

Phase II dialogue agenda and helped inform our theory of change. Finally, it is impossible to sufficiently capture the level of excitement that dialogue participants expressed for their respective communities. Although the Council on South Sudanese American Relations thoroughly understands the strength of community dialogue, part of the effort is to encourage the support of ARCSS. CoSSAR team works tirelessly to connect members and community leaders to deeply engaged in support for peace and democracy in South Sudan. We encourage our community leaders to explore new ways of building partnerships with leaders of other tribes and collectively support peace in South Sudan. As a foundation, The Council on South Sudanese American Relations (CoSSAR) plans to support all diaspora community leaders in order to give peace a chance in South Sudan.

In order to find ways to align diaspora voices and make a more significant impact in bringing people to people reconciliation, these community dialogues will continue to convene throughout the US. The diaspora dialogue will continue to be a meaningful platform for interaction between members of different communities and is an essential ingredient that ignites a culture of peace and reconciliation in our country. These dialogue and civil conversations are vital to breaking down barriers that divide the diaspora community. All who attended these gatherings in this process expressed appreciation for meaningful conversations around trauma health, reconciliation, and peace in South Sudan.

A Photograph of Whispers Between Rugged Mud Walls

BY Marial Awendit

Wholly cured of indecisions,
Dreams packed and a cigar lit,
I wait if the rugged mud walls
Will womb me in.
All those nine months,
If I had workable suspicions
They were all plotting
To scrub delight off tree barks,
The universe may again take
His voice
To
weave fire   into a flower.
Hands.
Cuddle.
Whichever,
I shall still hug the night,
My hands light as
God's
Searching for Himself
In a sack overflowing with mud.

My hands cupping whispers,
He may know
When I collect basketfuls
Of true pain and
sculpt it into a statue,
Just like I plot to
pour emptiness
Out of clay pots.
He may know how between flooded days
Laid with broken bridges,
When full of myself I can still float,
Earth under my feet
Still coarse to wash down
With things
rinsed in syrups.

GIVING SOUTH SUDAN A SPORTING CHANCE

There is no question, South Sudan has produced many talented athletes. The civil wars resulting in our independence helped to produce an interest in sports. Many young men and women who were displaced and who became refugees in Ethiopia and Kenya learned to play football (soccer) and basketball in the camps. Athletics not only helped young people to keep busy but they helped develop self-discipline, team spirit, and a determination to excel.

Those who remained in their home villages were in some ways less lucky. They didn't learn to play sports but continued playing traditional games. As the government in Khartoum moved towards Islamic fundamentalism and pushed sharia law, the opportunity to enjoy sports became even less in the areas that they controlled.

While South Sudanese athletes excel in many sports including track and field and wrestling as well as football and basketball, it has been in the latter sport that our nation has been most noticed by the rest of the world. Starting with Manute Bol, our people have contributed a number of outstanding players to the NBA and the WNBA.

Current South Sudanese professional basketball players include Adut Bulgak who was drafted by the New York Liberty in 2016. In the NBA, Luol Deng, Thon Maker, and Deng Adel are already playing; others are in the developmental leagues and are expected to soon join the big leagues.

Also, South Sudan has produced some outstanding track and field starts. Going back to 2008, when Lopez Lomong was a flag bearer for the United States, our countrymen and women have been making their mark in the sport.

In Australia our brothers and sisters are breaking recored. Here in the states Athiang Mou, whose name is sometimes spelled Athing Mu, has been setting records in the 600 meters.

The growth of sport in our culture and especially back home in our country is important. It is not only a source of pride but a force for solidarity. Athletes can become heroes and role-models for our children.

The fervor with which our children in South Sudan support soccer teams from England demonstrates that sport has an emotional force akin to religion. As such, it has great potential for good.

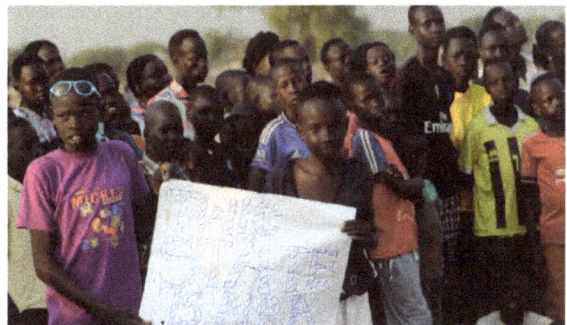

SOMEDAY SOON OUR CHILDREN...

Someday,and hopefully soon, our children and other children from and of Africa will be playing sports developed in our own homelands.

After all, soccer, basketball,even most track and field events were developed someplace.

In some cases, for example basketball and volleyball, a specific person decided to create a game.

Now those games are played around the world. As the nations of Africa grown and develop, hopefully some of our athletes and recreation leaders will work to create new sports, sports that reflect the cultures of our continent.

In the meantime, we of South Sudan can stand tall knowing that our athletes are making a mark for themselves and our country on the world sporting stage.

Deng Fanan: A Tribute

By Deng Mayik Atem

Deng Kuot Thiech, known by South Sudanese and most of the world as Deng Fanan, was a dear friend and a great inspiration. He died on Saturday, July 5, 2019. His music provided a link to our culture no matter where we were. His songs sharpened our thinking and imagination, and reminded us of the heroes who struggled so that South Sudan might be free.

His music ranged from traditional, church, Guerrllia moral songs, to political. Deng's music continues to connect us to past political and spiritual leaders, and reminds us of our country's struggle and those who made great contributions. His humility and humor made him a loved figure who was listened to for his messages as well as his music; messages of encouragement to carry us through hard times.

I saw Deng Fanan perform several times in Pinyudo, but I met him when Dr. John Garang visited the camp in 1990. How we roared when Deng took the stage and with great energy we sang along -- his songs electrifying and motivating us all. As he sang and we joined in, John Garang nodded his head in approval, keeping time to the music. At that moment, Deng Fanan's music touched the soul of our cause and assured us that a solution was possible.

In December, 1992, Deng Fanan stopped by our house in Kakuma. I was living with Paul Akech Deng at the time, and Deng came was carrying a pair of trousers on his shoulder. "I have to take these to the market. The zipper is broken," he told us. I took the trousers and fixed the zipper, which impressed him.

He started to talk with me, telling me that he had visited my area some years before. But we discovered he had the wrong area because he thought I came from Twic Bor in Jonglei.

"Makur, Deng Columbus is from Gogrial and he's your nasip," Uncle Akech Deng interjected. After that, Deng Fanan called me MaColumbo. Always there was affection and a hint of laughter in his voice.

I last saw Deng in December 2018 when I stopped by his residence in Gogrial. I had returned to South Sudan to help register Ramciel Magazine and wanted to see my friend and inspiration.

Deng Fanan was a bit put out that I hadn't given him advance notice. "You are my favorite son, MaColumbo, and it would have been nice for you to spend the night here with me."

I apologized and suggested that on my next visit I would stay a few days. I also hoped that he would show me around and tell me more about the local historical sites. Sadly, I will never have the chance to spend that time with my dear friend. He is gone.

God gives and God takes. We cannot bring Deng Fanan back. We can, however, remember him and recognize his contribution to our country and our culture. It was right and proper for our nation's president to escort Deng Fanan's body to the airport to be taken to the burial site in his home village. I could not be there that day, but I know the next time I am in South Sudan I will visit his grave. Perhaps I will bring a pair of pants for him.

"My dear Uncle Deng Kuot, you were unique. Your warmth, humility, humor, talent, and national pride remain an inspiration to all South Sudanese." That is a song worth singing to a man who has departed this world but will always be in my heart.

DON'T CRY FOR ME!

By Adhar Dor Mayar

Don't cry for me. I will be
okay, Our memories are my home now,
And that's where I will
stay.

Don't cry for me. I'm where
I belong, a ruin! I want you to be happy,
And try to stay strong and
calm.

Don't cry for me. It was
just our perfect time, but I will see you someday
On the other side, the
physical world.

Don't cry for me. I am not
alone, the memories you left are with me,
They welcome me home and
greet me every time I make a move.

Don't cry for me. For I
have no fear, all my pain is gone
And the world took my
tears, I was accommodated!

Don't cry for me. This is
not the end. I will be waiting here for you,
When we meet again.

Don't cry for me. I always
carry you in my heart, my memory still holds you firm
I will store you in my
soul.

Don't cry for me. My skin
may not be right for you, but in my memory you are safe
I will protect our little
secrets.

Don't cry for me. Because
when I first met you, no human knew
you would make it into my sacred soul
I carried you!

Don't cry for me. I remember our little walks
that nobody liked or paid attention to,
I know I left you out at the cold streets
I wanted you protected!

Don't cry for me.
Because we had a talk and agreed that we would
protect each other from us I let your flesh go
but your being is domicile in my memory.

Don't cry for me.
I will choose you, even when you my me feel hurt
My love for you won't fade simply because I placed you
in my memory And not on my skin!

Don't cry for me.
I know I got frustrated over my several fights for you
I still go to a battle for you, I have not forgotten
all the beautiful things you brought my way!

Don't cry for me.
I will choose you, still choose you
And keep choosing you every single day with every single breath
Left in me. I will choose you because you are made for everyone
But not everyone was made for you I will choose you
because you are not human
And you didn't hurt me that much!
MY DREAMS!!!!

THE WOMAN OF STEEL PEACE AMBASSADOR. To the South Sudanese and the country in general, please let's listen to the mute souls and look for people who are fighting for their dreams to come true, let's uplift one another as the great KUSH people and stop categorizing ourselves.We are too great for that.We are being taken advantage of not because we are the youngest nation in the world but because we like paying attention to what destroys us more than what brings us together. Let's have integrity and solidarity. It's our responsibility to bring our people back home and bring our home back to its feet. We want to walk again on the beautiful, solid ground we belong to and call it our own. Let's us love us and be unique as God created us. The tall intelligent beautiful dark skinned people. I LOVE ROSS TO THE MAXIMUM!!

SCOOP IT!

Where the News from the Diaspora and South Sudan Meet!

Kon Andrew Deng a.k.a. Andrews Kays

A South Sudanese artist based in Uganda, Mr. Kays started his music career in 2015 with the first song titled Ana Taban. His music had transcended beyond Juba, especially with his recent breakthrough song called Tell Me.

Grace Bol

Miss Grace Bol graced the cover of Ramciel Magazine's first edition. She is a South Sudanese-American with an iconic fashion and style who uses her influence in positive way. Her supporters and fans are the inspiration behind everything she does.

William Akoi Mawwin

William Akoi Mawwin Antislavery Usable Past

SCOOP IT!

Where the News from the Diaspora and South Sudan Meet!

Ustaz Awut Mayom Agok, Educator

Ms. Agok is from Hope and Resurrection Secondary School in Rumbek, Western Lake State. She has been one of the few South Sudanese female educators who are currently teaching and directing one of the secondary schools in South Sudan.

Empowering and educating girls in South Sudan must be a priority, because educated women raise healthy and smart families. Let us honor and celebrate our women as they are the foundation of our society. The future is a female.

Achai Bol Giir

Giir, a.k.a. Queen of the River Nile. Miss Achai Bol Giir is a South Sudanese-Canadian actress, artist, and a model-based in Toronto, Ontario. Miss Achai Bol Giir graduated from the acting school, where she studied Acting for Voice and camera, and she also graduated from Law, Security, and Police Foundations, and also she is former 2010-2011 Miss South Sudan USA's, First Princess. Nhier Du Amit, is Achai's latest song, and it had been phenomenal on YouTube.

South Sudan Enters The Age of Robotics...

A team of South Sudanese high school students mentored by Richard Ring Kuach, took part in the FIRST Global Robotic competition held in Washington DC in 2017, Mexico in 2018, Dubai in 2019. The team won a gold medal for courageous achievement in 2017 Washington DC's FIRST Global Challenge. That award recognized the challenges the team faced building their robot name RamcielBotic. RamcielBotic was designed and built with the aim and purpose, to clean our dirty environment, generate electricity to save our environment from pollution, clean our ocean, lakes, rivers in order to save aquatic life.

Mr. Kuach was also honored as the best mentor, one who never gave up despite challenges the team faced in 2017 competition. "Knowing is not enough," Mr. Kuach told the competitors; "the knowledge acquired must be applied to solve real world problems.

Being willing is not enough, but we must do to solve the problem." With a moto like that, no wonder he is an inspiration to students. Neither doing or winning has come easily to Mr. Kuach. He has worked hard to acquire a good education. After completing his primary school at Marial-Lou Comboni Primary School in Tonj North in 2006, In 2007 he attended John Paul II Secondary School in Wau, where he focused on science.

At that point, his goal was medical studies, and he was accepted at the University of Bhar El Ghazel Wau in 2011. However, he changed his plans and went to study a B.Sc. in computer engineering from Cavendish University in 2015. In 2017 he went for further studies to pursue an M.S. in engineering specializing in electronic information and communication engineering at Huazhong University of Science and Technology.

Mr. Kuach has become an expert in the research necessary for future wireless networking based on edge cloud computing and in automatous robotics.

The South Sudan Robotics Team, is supported by FIRST Global Community, an American-based NGO in Washington DC. Mr. Kuach aims to mobilize and encourage South Sudanese youth from the age of 18 years and below to join and participate in Science, Technology, Engineering and Mathematics (STEM).

The study of STEM subjects' gears students to innovation and creativity in solving real world problems. As such, these young robotics engineers applied the skills acquired through STEM to represent the promise of our nation's young people and their ability to contribute in the development of our country. Technology boosts production and encourages progress in various fields.

Currently most of the population uses generators as the source of energy instead of using hydropower or renewable energy such solar power, which would help us fight environmental pollution caused by the use of diesel and fuel and plastic bottles, Every Year, Team South Sudan Robotic put in more effort which earned them another opportunity to participate and compete in 2018 Mexico, 2019 Dubai FIRST Global Challenge.

Mr. Kuach is currently a lecturer in University of Juba, school of Computer Science and & IT, and he is also a mentor of FIRST Global Team South Sudan at STEM Centre afflicted to University of Juba. He started working with FIRST Global Organization since 2017. You can reach the FIRST GLOBAL TEAM SOUTH SUDAN at **http://bit.ly/2Ns4wH2**

SCOOP IT!

Where the News from the Diaspora and South Sudan Meet!

Mr. Makuach Ajing Chol, William Gaui, Luol Deng, Margaret Wol, and Chol Ring Bol

Former NBA Star Luol Deng in Phoenix with President of the South Sudanese Community Mr. Makuach Ajing Chol, William Gaui, Maragret Wol, and Chol Ring Bol (2018)

David D. Achuoth, Miss Mohajer, and Daniel Atem

Executive Director and co-founder of Council on South Sudanese American Relations Mr. David D. Achuoth, Miss. Mohajer (Program Assistant for Africa Program at USIP, and Daniel Atem of CoSSAR during South Sudan Diaspora Dialogue in Washington D.C at the USIP July 2019.

SCOOP IT!

Where the News from the Diaspora and South Sudan Meet!

Akout John Mangok & Adhar Dor Mayar

In Nairobi, Kenya representing with Traditional Beading.

Artists Deng Abuk & Jackline Achuei Deng Ajing

South Sudanese Artists Deng Abuk & Jackline Achuei Deng Ajing during Ring Machakos' Album Luanch in Juba(2019).

Artist Daniel Dinganyai

Artist Daniel Dinganyai in Phoenix AZ during his 2015 USA Tour.

SCOOP IT!

Where the News from the Diaspora and South Sudan Meet!

Kakuma Refugee Camp

Coop from 2018-2019 Kakuma Refugee camp in North Kenya - Photo by Ajak Dau

Atongoya Guot

Comedian, actress, singer, and a beautiful woman of many talents, Atongoya is Founder of SSOLLYWOOD GLOBAL PRODUCTION

Bakhita Longar

Alumnus of University of Nairobi, model, actress. As an alumnus of the University of Nairobi, and a South Sudanese model and actress with Ssollywood Global Production, Miss Longar is not just only a pretty face, but an intellectual as well.

SCOOP IT!

Where the News from the Diaspora and South Sudan Meet!

Rapper Hot Dogg

Rapper Hot Dogg & Biggie at Luol Deng Foundation's South Sudan Unite on July 2019 in Phoenix

Deng Angok & Amekjang Madak

Deng Angok and Amekjang Madak in Phoenix, Arizona during Ramciel Mgazine's online edition lauch.

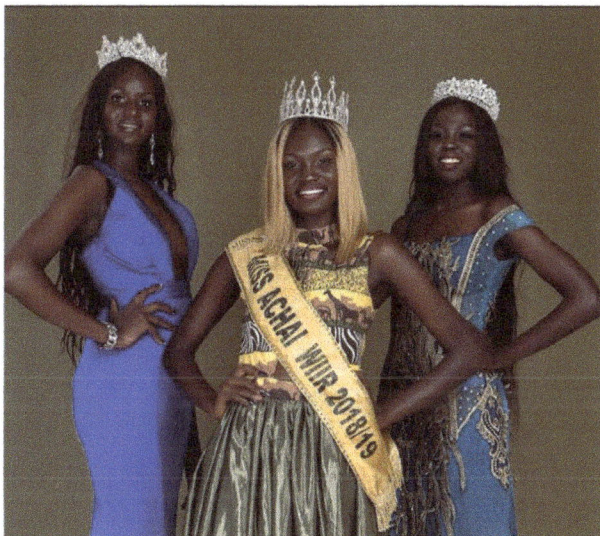

Winners of Miss Achai Wiir 2018-2019

Winners of Miss Achai Wiir 2018-2019 Miss Jeena Manut with by 1st Runner Athiei Atem and Miss Mariah Nyayeina Joseph during Miss Achai Wiir Beauty Pageant show in Juba.

IN HONOR OF OUR COFFEE COUNTRY! 734 COFFEE IS BORN

We Have More Than 12 Million Reason...

We have more than 12 million reasons why it's time for us to show our appreciation for the people of South Sudan. During our 30 years of war we had help and support from friends and allies from all over the world and we are extremely appreciative.

A wedding is a ceremony where two people are united in marriage. Wedding traditions and customs vary greatly between cultures, ethnic groups, religions, countries, and social classes

Moreover; the steadfast love and support that we have received from our country is the fuel that keeps us going. Our mission is to grant everyone the opportunity to taste 734 Coffee and now we have the responsibility to recognize the South Sudanese people by introducing 734 Coffee Peace Blend for South Sudan.

We strive for world peace and we accomplish this through development and Education.

734 Coffee sells delicious coffee to U.S. consumers in order to provide college scholarships to refugees of South Sudan.

734 Coffee is growing, this inspires more organizations to focus on the forgotten people Sudan. It encourages businesses to seriously consider Sudan as a place where business is possible and its people as good businessmen and women.

BUSINESS GROWTH...

There are an enormous number of youth organizations in Sudan vying for support to grow, with little to none, their energies will dwindle over time if they don't see a fruitful future.

For 734 coffee To be recognized on the international platform, translates to opportunity for growth. South Sudan has had a difficult recent past, but this is not the future that we see for the region. Every connection means an opportunity for value creation,and Through entrepreneurship, the young people of south Sudan can create a desirable future for themselves.

734 Coffee was founded on the idea of entrepreneurship, and the value of building for future generations.

When the people of South Sudan are able to sustain and see growth in their lives, the stability of the region is inevitable, and only then will peace be viable.

RAMCIEL

Miss Mariah Nyayiena Joseph

www.ramcielmagazine.com

2020 MEDIA KIT

ONLINE AD UNITS

LEADERBOARD 728 X 90

FULL BANNER

480 X 60

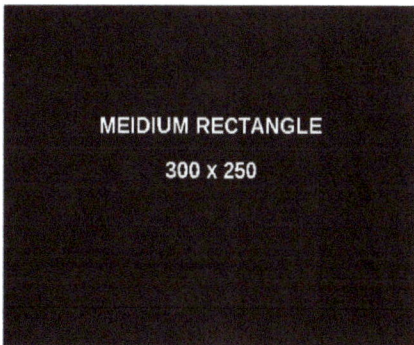

MEIDIUM RECTANGLE

300 x 250

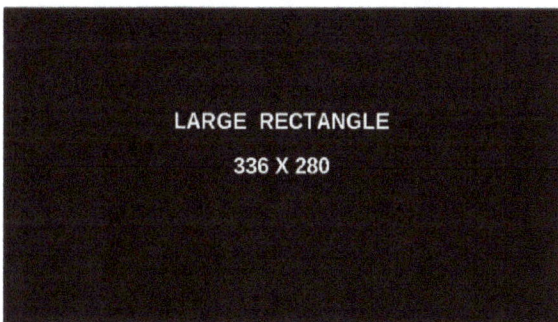

LARGE RECTANGLE

336 X 280

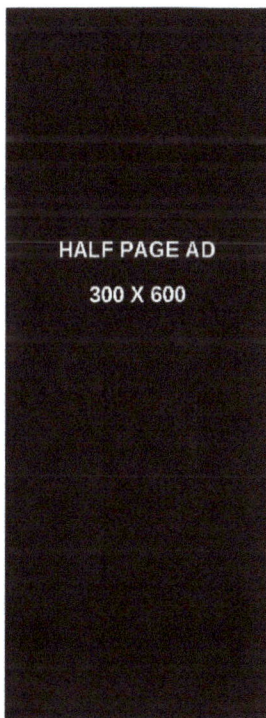

HALF PAGE AD

300 X 600

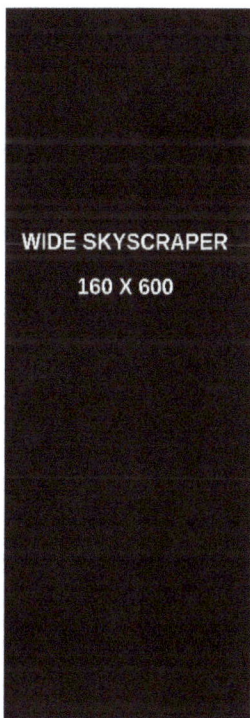

WIDE SKYSCRAPER

160 X 600

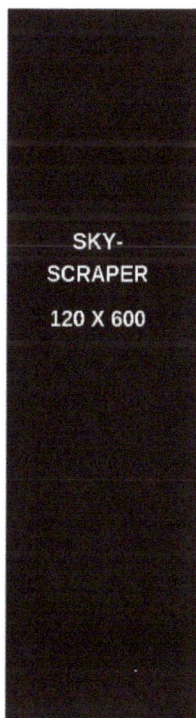

SKY-SCRAPER

120 X 600

RAMCIEL ONLINE MAGAZINE

AD SPACES

HARD COPY AD UNITS

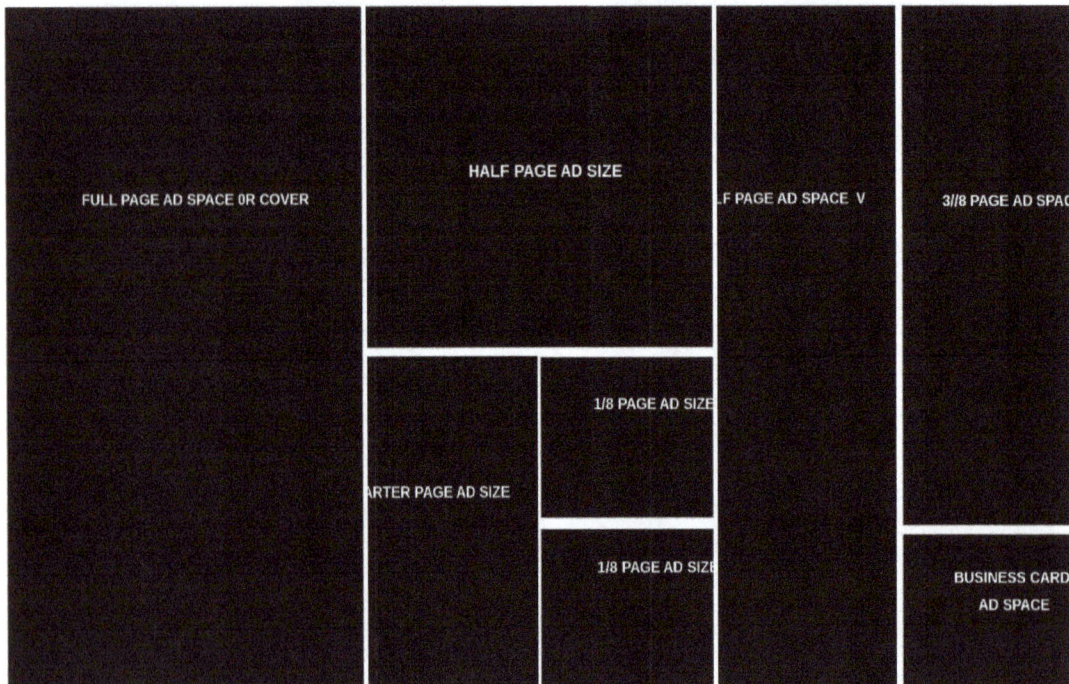

FULL PAGE AD SPACE 0R COVER

HALF PAGE AD SIZE

LF PAGE AD SPACE V

3//8 PAGE AD SPAC

1/8 PAGE AD SIZE

ARTER PAGE AD SIZE

1/8 PAGE AD SIZE

BUSINESS CARD
AD SPACE

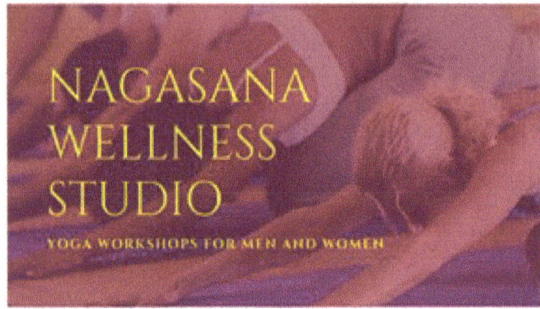

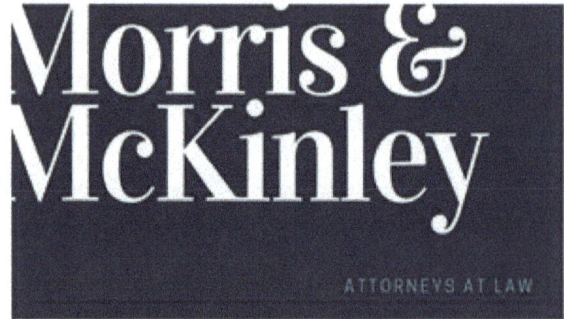

Our Staff

Publisher Deng Mayik Atem - USA

Editor in Chief Kenneth Weene - USA

Senior Christy White - USA

Editor: Madit D. Ring Yel - USA

Staff Writer Asara Bullen - Juba, South Sudan

Staff Writer Adhieu Majok - London UK

Contributing Writer Marko Makat - Juba, South Sudan

Photographer Tino Matoc Deng Mangok -Juba, South Sudan
Photographer K Pesa Cuts - Juba, South Sudan
Photographer Dani'Lee - Juba, South Sudan
Photographer Chris 4D - Juba, South Sudan

Nyuonville: Nairobi, Kenya

Photographer Ajak Dau - USA
Photographer Adhar Dor Mayar - Nairobi Kenya

Contributors Chol Ayuen, Thuch Ajak, Marko Makat

Art/Graphics/Magazine Formatting - Vertikal Media Group USA/3 E Web Media Manchester UK

EDITORIAL OFFICES

PHOENIX, AZ UNITED STATES
CONTACT NUMBER: 1.602.348.2650

JUBA, SOUTH SUDAN
CONTACT NUMBER: 2.119.773.1641

WWW.RAMCIELMAGAZINE.COM
iINFO@RAMCIELMAGAZINE.COM

RAMCIEL

SERVING THE PEOPLE OF SOUTH SUDAN

FOLLOW US   @RAMCIELMAGAZINE